The
Vile Practices
of Church
Leadership

Finance and
Administration

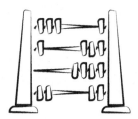

Nate Berneking

Nashville

THE VILE PRACTICES OF CHURCH LEADERSHIP:
FINANCE AND ADMINISTRATION

Copyright © 2017 by Abingdon Press

This book is printed on acid-free paper.

Library of Congress Cataloging-in-Publication Data has been requested.

ISBN: 978-1-5018-1896-7

17 18 19 20 21 22 23 24 25 26   10 9 8 / 6 5 4 3 2 1

MANUFACTURED IN THE UNITED STATES OF AMERICA

Contents

Contents

Introduction

At four in the afternoon I submitted to be more vile, and proclaimed in the highways the glad tidings of salvation.

—John Wesley

On April 2, 1739, apparently at the specific hour of 4 p.m., John Wesley decided to set aside his own preferences and interact with people who weren't attending worship, men and women toiling in mines or fields, laboring in trades, drinking in pubs, living ordinary lives, often in squalid conditions. The notion of preaching in fields or meetinghouses, rather than churches, seemed so culturally and religiously uncouth that he, an ordained priest, a member of a "higher" class set apart from peasants, tradespeople, and workers, resisted. Yet his own need to share the good news with *all* people overwhelmed his sensibilities.

Submitting to be more vile, he embraced field preaching, class organizing, and in the end, even ordaining preachers and superintendents for America, an act of explicit disobedience to his bishop, all as the means to support one priority: sharing the gospel. This is the way of life in any mission field. In order to yield fruit, we must be ready to be more vile, to set aside sensibilities and declare sharing the gospel as our priority.

United Methodists are steeped in the mission field metaphor, an understanding that the communities in which we work need translation and enculturation. As pastors and laity, we must set aside sensibilities and preferences to prioritize the gospel. Ideally, church leaders work to learn the appropriate strategies for sharing the gospel even when those strategies take them outside their preferences.

In recent years, many American Christians have come to understand pastoral leadership in terms of an ability to strategize for evangelism. One might even say evangelistic strategizing has become the central pastoral activity, changing what it means to be in pastoral ministry and requiring us to be more intentional in outreach efforts. Unfortunately, not every area necessary for reaching new generations has been addressed so intentionally.

I. Stating the Issue

I'd like to use this book to draw attention to one lagging area, to a set of practices many prefer to ignore, while others dread having to consider. Many of the same pastors who adeptly strategize in matters of evangelism, faith formation, and mission activities, likewise exhibit fear and ignorance when considering matters of finance and administration. Despite extensive literature relating to stewardship and generosity, many even struggle with those activities, while finance and administrative practices are left unaddressed. Yet, effective ministry practices must be undergirded by healthy practices of budgeting, accounting, and financial reporting. The truth is, given the reluctance to explore finance and administration with greater intentionality, many pastors have never even been presented with the opportunity to grasp the most basic skills.

I use *finance and administration* as a shorthand for a huge range of topics that touch upon congregational life: budgeting, accounting, retirement savings/pensions, other employee benefits, staff management, real-estate matters, and other general legal issues. It isn't that authors have failed to make the connections between generosity and a congregation's administrative health. Instead, many pastors simply haven't been able or willing to submit to the *vileness* necessary to learn these skills.

Many aren't even able to take that step to improve their personal financial practices. With the rest of the population, student debt and poor financial planning nag clergy. Any financial, legal, or administrative issue has the potential to strike fear in the hearts of faithful and otherwise competent pastors. As a result, pastors often leave the finances and administration of their local churches to laity who are equally fearful and ignorant of how such practices ought to be conducted at church. Laity may be well versed in business, but struggle to make translations needed for Christian communities, lacking spiritual language or United Methodist particularities, feeling self-conscious in matters they pursue with confidence at work or home.

If we are to support our priorities in ministry, pastors and laity need more resources and greater clarity when it comes to finance and administration.

II. Basic Assumptions: Holy People for Holy Congregations

Before we get too far, I confess to certain assumptions, some the subject of vigorous, even healthy debate. For example, I take for granted that the Church must develop local congregations with an ability to translate things usually understood as secular into inherently spiritual language. I embrace the notion that Christians must always move from their congregations into the communities around them. I further embrace the notion that sharing the gospel is the world's greatest hope for transformation and healing. This movement and sharing is always the central task of Christians and local churches. In other words, I embrace Wesley's priority of sharing the gospel.

These assumptions about the central task of churches shape my understanding of congregational leadership. All people are called to ministry, but pastors and some laity are set apart for a unique task with two parts: leading the congregation to share the good news with the communities around them, and strengthening those in the congregation who conduct that work.

From the beginning, Jesus sent his disciples, the spiritual leaders of the early movement, with "power and authority" to share that "God's kingdom" was near and to offer healing to broken people (Luke 9:1-10). They were sent as holy and empowered people to share a holy message. That's still the central task. Secondarily, leaders were charged with strengthening those doing the sharing. In Acts 14, the Holy Spirit sent the newly converted Apostle Paul to several towns and villages. Paul and Barnabas visited the cities of Iconium and Lystra. They did just as the first disciples in Luke 9. They shared the good news. People were intrigued, even converted. Then, Paul and Barnabas moved elsewhere. In the last verses of 14, however, they *returned* to Iconium and Lystra and "strengthened the disciples and urged them to remain firm in the faith" (v. 22). They also "appointed elders for each church" (v. 23). In other words, the model set forth by the early Christians was to proclaim the message and then, to establish communities to assist people in keeping and sharing the faith.

This was John Wesley's model. He preached in the fields gaining converts, then organized people into classes and societies. He sent his preachers to those societies to do just as Paul did in Lystra and Iconium: to strengthen souls and encourage people.

The Church has always needed the work of both evangelists and leaders entrusted with the work of soul strengthening. Pastors lead in both roles, and the trust required for it has never come cheaply.

The Apostle Paul was at his best when his churches trusted his intentions and motivations. When trust was eroded, his work became more difficult. When United Methodist pastors lose the trust of their congregations, regardless of a pastor's guilt or innocence, a conversation with the district superintendent is almost certain to come.

From Jesus and his early disciples to Paul to John Wesley and now in our era, pastors and certain laity are understood in terms of a *holy people* sent to lead *holy communities*, communities charged with the task of sharing the good news, thereby transforming the world. People don't have to be perfect for this role, ordination vows notwithstanding, but we must always maintain integrity with our congregations. If pastors call for holy living such that the greater community might develop its own trust of the congregation, the members of that congregation must always be assured that the pastor engages in the same patterns of holy living. Pastors must keep priorities straight, even when it means acting in ways they feel are "vile." Without a clear and firmly rooted priority for the good news, without living into behaviors consistent with that priority, calls of hypocrisy will grow louder, always nagging, hindering ministry.

Leaders must constantly strive to maintain their own personal and social holiness in order to retain their authority to lead congregations in their quest for the same personal and social holiness. It's a bit too simple to say that they must lead by good example, but practicing what one preaches is simply the basic cost of doing ministry.

In each generation, this has meant something different. In our own era, much emphasis is placed on strategy, facilitation of resources, and administrative oversight. With these emphases, it is troubling that pastors (not to mention laity leaders) struggle in matters of personal finance and administration, a struggle that manifests in personal *and* congregational life. Finance and administration are key aspects of healthy communities in the eyes of many. And, too many congregations lack meaningful spiritual leadership when it comes to budgeting, accounting, managing resources, and facilitating generosity. When leaders are unable to provide effective leadership with respect to finances, the whole congregation begins to erode in its effectiveness. The perception of outsiders may be worse. When a pastor is unable to lead through times of financial concern or conflicted budget processes, the congregation loses sight of the real purpose of financial resources. Blind to these purposes, a congregation's ability to discern the work to which it is called erodes, unsettling the very ground on which it builds shared life.

I contend that learning basic financial and administrative skills, something considered vile by so many, becomes a gateway on the path to holiness, and therefore a means toward individual and congregational discernment of actual ministry. Learning how to care for one's God-given resources is part of what it is to listen for what God might desire.

III. Addressing the Issue: Becoming More Vile to Be More Holy

This book's purpose is twofold: (a) to provide a primer on several financial and administrative matters; and (b) to articulate a basic theological understanding of the work around finance and administration. Despite the lack of intentionality, I've found an audience aware of the need for integrity and starving for information that would help them achieve it. Most leaders want to be healthier in matters of finance and administration, even as they resist it. It is important to articulate these matters in a manner consistent with the polity of The United Methodist Church.

Beyond the pragmatic, pastors must develop an ability to translate. As Christians, we live in a world with two realms. On the one hand, we operate in the ecclesiastical realm. In The United Methodist Church, we are comfortable with the language of conferencing, sacraments, and Scripture. We speak easily of discipleship processes, even when we aren't sure what they ought to be. We use the language of prayer, and theologically, we deploy eschatological terms to discuss the Church's purpose. We believe God is "transforming the world" and at least our clergy can talk about their work and the work of their churches in those terms. We're even well versed in language that at first blush seems administrative: the *Book of Discipline*, church council, trustees, finance, charge conference, and end-of-year reports.

At the same time, the world we inhabit has a second realm, one that understands itself as secular. It isn't that no one believes in God anymore. But, in this realm, people, some even attending church, fail to articulate the connection of things in this secular realm to any sort of divinity, higher power, or God. Pastors certainly inhabit this realm, and in some matters, move easily in and out of the ecclesiastical and secular. On their best days, pastors even articulate a theological vision that encompasses both: one world, created by God, but broken and at least partially separated from the God seeking to redeem the whole thing.

In matters of finance, however, pastors and lay leaders struggle (a) to understand the secular language and approach, (b) to comprehend how those secular approaches might interface with ecclesiastical structures, and (c) to translate both the secular and their own ecclesiastical knowledge into terms that will facilitate health in their congregations. I want to offer the basics of the language of finance and administration while also articulating a theological understanding. I want to offer theological language that might be used when thinking through and translating these matters for a Christian community.

I've broken the book into two parts. In part I, I sketch out practices for the personal finances of pastors and other church leaders. I do this out of the conviction that it takes people striving to be more holy, to lead holy congregations. I don't want to be misunderstood as holding leaders to an unattainable standard of perfection. Rather, I seek only to encourage colleagues to be more vile: to be better, more informed, and more consistent with their own financial behavior. I've shaped the chapters around topics about which I am asked most frequently—personal generosity, personal budgeting, retirement savings (specifically United Methodist pension programs), and planning for taxes. I begin with personal generosity, a practice pastors are often quite good at fulfilling, many much better than me. My intent is to articulate how generosity might flow through all other financial practices.

In part II, I transition from writing of holy people to discussing matters in the congregations they lead. Churches always want to know how to "get more money." I just don't have the answer. Instead, I offer ways of talking about generosity that I believe are more compelling than others. I'm aware that churches believe they need more money, but that's grounded in fear about the future. I advocate an approach to finances shaped by the courage and trust required for great acts of generosity. Using trust as the central theme, I move on to matters of budgeting, accounting, basic tax, and a few legal issues.

I'm not naïve. This book will not end anxiety in matters of finance and administration. Instead, I hope to offer a starting point. Even limited changes can yield results. Readers can find more information on each of the chapters, together with additional resources, sample documents, and questions for reflection at the website www.nateberneking.com. With this book and the additional resources, I hope that pastors and laity who see finance and administration as the nastiest parts of congregational life will, with Wesley, submit to be more vile. I hope they gain more traction in leadership; I hope they find themselves a holy people leading holy congregations.

PART I

Holy People

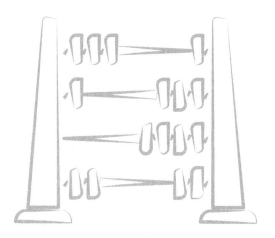

Chapter 1

Personal Generosity: Developing an Open Posture

Good financial and administrative practices begin with generosity. Lived out by faithful leaders, taking any one of a variety of forms, generosity lies at the root of good things happening in local churches. If we desire better financial leadership, we must begin by seeking more generosity.

I'll mostly refer to financial generosity, but all good things find their source in people who give, however it might be expressed. A generous approach to life, what I call an *open posture*, undergirds everything that follows in this book. Bishop Robert Schnase wrote of the need for leaders to characterize their ministries by "saying yes."[1] What he meant by that and what I mean by an open posture or living with a generous spirit, are the same. Christians do their best work, regardless of what it might be, when they face the world with a generous, permission-giving, open posture. We speak of being selfless or sacrificial. We encourage "extravagant generosity" and

1. Robert Schnase, *Just Say Yes! Unleashing People for Ministry* (Nashville: Abingdon, 2015).

"risk-taking mission and service."[2] When we say these things, we acknowledge that Christian work is an outflow of ourselves for the benefit of others. We express the need for a generous, open posture in ministry. Finance and administration are no different.

I. Practices and Patterns of Individual Generosity

To be effective, a pastor or leader must work to master four areas of generosity. Two of these lie well beyond the mission and ministry of the church he or she happens to be serving. That may bother Christians committed to the exclusivity of financial giving to the local church. I've had to come to terms with it myself. In fact, I'll be the first to admit that I haven't always done well maintaining generosity in all four areas. Giving to the local church has been easy. I was raised to do so, but in most other matters, I've often tried to express a charming sense of frugality. I've claimed that frugality in the name of my family of origin (one part Southern, Depression-era America and one part German immigrant).

The truth is, when I've failed at being generous, I've simply failed. There was no charm about it. I wasn't frugal. I was greedy, and when that happened, my ministry suffered. I suffered, not in some supernatural connection to God's disfavor or reciprocal justice, so much as the hard-to-swallow fact that miserliness in one part of life quickly spreads to others. And, miserliness is never appreciated, loved, or respected. Anytime I've failed to give, I've lost respect. So, I say unequivocally, hard as it is, frightening as it is:

2. Robert Schnase, *Five Practices of Fruitful Congregations* (Nashville: Abingdon, 2007), 7.

effective church leaders must master generosity, of which there are four types: (1) generosity to support the mission of one's local church; (2) generosity to the local church beyond general giving; (3) generosity to organizations and efforts in the outside community; and (4) general, day-in-and-day-out generosity.

Generosity to Support the Mission of the Local Church

Must I tithe? No matter how many authors and consultants have insisted that the answer is yes, I still get the question. At times, for ease and convenience, I've simply answered: Yes, you have to tithe.

I wish it *were* that simple. After all, explaining the tithe, at its heart, is pretty easy. Don't ask 10 percent of what. Just start with 10 percent of something. Call it "income." We figure out what we make and multiply it by .1. Then we write a regular and consistent check—monthly, biweekly, weekly, it doesn't matter. If we make $75,000 a year, that's $7,500. Divide $7,500 by 52 if you give weekly or 12, if monthly.

All the preachers and consultants are correct when they direct people away from the amount given and toward what they have left after they do. Giving 10 percent of $75,000 leaves one with $67,500 on which to live. For most in the middle class, especially pastors receiving income-tax-free housing, tithing is affordable. Yes, we must tithe to be effective.

I wish it really was that simple. My mind just won't allow it to be, but maybe not in the way you think. Certainly we can find a semblance of the 10 percent figure in Scripture. But, what about the story of the rich young ruler? Jesus doesn't say to him, "There's just one more thing. Make sure you give 10 percent of your income to the church (or maybe synagogue . . . or maybe to Jesus himself)." Jesus said, "There's one more thing. Sell everything you own and distribute the money to the poor. Then you will have treasure in heaven. And come, follow me" (Luke 18:22).

Then, there's Zacchaeus (Luke 19:1-10). Yes, he climbed a tree, and Jesus invited himself to Zacchaeus's house, but Jesus *didn't* tell him to tithe. Nor did Zacchaeus insist he was already giving 10 percent of his income. Zacchaeus actually told Jesus, and hence the reader, that he was already giving *half.* For anyone, like me who's still unable to focus, stuck thinking about the young ruler told to give everything, that's only 50 percent; *only* 50 percent.

Scripture ties quite a knot when it comes to wealth and generosity. We need to untie it, though the consequences may be less than desirable for many. In Luke, Jesus didn't say, "Blessed are those who give 10 percent of their income to the church." He said, "Blessed are the poor" or in the Common English Bible, "Happy are you who are poor" (Luke 6:20). Worse, he offered an accompanying "woe," indicating "how terrible" it was for any who were "rich." Why? For they'd received their consolation or comfort; they'd already received what they believed to be needed to make their life better (Luke 6:24). The poor don't have any consolation. Because of this, they are apt to turn to the only place that *actually* offers consolation, the God who created and desires to redeem all things.

This is the nugget that explains what Jesus was getting at with Zacchaeus and the rich young ruler. Zacchaeus had overcome the false sense of consolation brought by wealth. He was disposing of the thing that had held him back from the life God would have people to live. The young ruler, on the other hand, was simply unable to make a true commitment. His wealth was too dear to him, too much a part of his identity to turn his attention and trust to an unseen God.

When we ask if we must tithe, we, as pastors, are asking the wrong question. As we'll see in the latter part of this chapter, Scripture, not to mention the traditions of the Church, makes it clear that all Christians, to truly follow Christ, must be willing to set aside everything that holds them back, that keeps them from committing their entire selves. For many, maybe most, money holds us back.

There is no expression of self about which we are touchier. If this is true, the question everyone must ask is, "How much must I give to make a full commitment of myself to Christ, to God, to the Church and its mission?" To answer, once set in that direction, one never quite stops until he or she gives everything. Generosity to the local church is part of a pattern of growth, from an initial step toward a complete commitment. Put another way, we must grow toward giving all of our resources for God's work. For pastors, that largely means our work in the local church. For laity, it may well mean both work in a local church and in other settings.

As much as I've always cringed to hear myself say it, to admit it to myself, 10 percent, at least for those of us without special circumstances, is probably just the floor. For those of us comfortable in our efforts to feed our families, especially for those of us able to spend on nonessentials, to give 10 percent is really just to get started in committing ourselves to what God might be doing through the Church and through our ministries.

That said, there may be another side, one that must be acknowledged if our call for tithing is to have any legitimacy. I truly believe that generosity, once started, can aid a person's decision making. At the same time, I am well aware that for some, giving

7

10 percent is a luxury that leaves much too little on which to live. If someone happens to be earning a salary near the poverty line, and it's combined with heavy obligations, especially those that weren't incurred intentionally, he or she is not excused from generosity, but the percentage of income such a person gives might be less.

Here's the test. If we have committed to true generosity, giving all we can financially, acting responsibly with respect to our spending, then the percentage of income that we give may vary from 1 percent to 99 percent depending on what that income actually is and how much is left for us after we make the gifts. If we're giving in that way, then we are already on our way to doing God's work in this world and through the Church. On the other hand, if we're tied up in knots worried about whether we have to give 10 percent of our income, or on what the 10 percent should be based, we've missed the point. I pray that anyone dealing with that sort of anxiety comes to a place of peace and takes a step of faith.

Yes, we have to tithe, but while some may be obligated to give less, I suspect many of us should do more. We are called to a full commitment of our resources to God's work. Part of God's work is the mission of the local churches we serve. If our church's ministry does not seem to be part of God's work in the world, then we shouldn't give to it. We shouldn't even be part of it. I've not experienced a local church about which I could say that. I've served dysfunctional churches as a layperson and pastor, but in all of them, beyond the dysfunctional behaviors, I held a deep conviction that the people, when gathered as the local church, were still doing God's work. They weren't perfect or even healthy, but, in general, they embodied God's work. It was to that embodiment that I wanted to commit.

Once one begins to tithe, I suspect more questions about giving to the local church may arise. One that puzzles both pastors and laity is, "Do I tell the rest of the congregation that I'm tithing?" That isn't easy to answer. Because a relationship grounded in trust is so critical to the pastor-parish relationship, I suggest pastors start by giving quietly. People will notice. It's more than okay to say, "My family and I have committed ourselves with a tithe." We can leave out the details. For laity, however, local churches may need and appreciate a more detailed witness to the experience with tithing. That isn't to say anyone needs to explain the amounts. Rather, talking about the journey to a certain level of generosity can be, and usually is, inspiring to others. When I've heard someone who's given a good witness to their generosity and what it's done for them spiritually and emotionally, I usually find myself wanting to join the generosity.

Yet, a witness about giving, whether from a pastor or from a lay leader, must always be done for the right reasons. Any utterance designed to manipulate or, worse, to draw attention to one's self, will do nothing but damage the greater Church. Personal witness to generosity must be done without bragging or expectation of increased power. The only appropriate reason to tell about one's own generosity is to give expression to what God is doing and what you hope God will do for others.

Consultants have long insisted that leaders must tithe in order to preserve their own integrity. I agree. Congregations just have a way of knowing when someone isn't practicing what they preach. When someone insists others should tithe without doing it themselves, they generate a rip in the fabric of congregational trust. But, there's more.

Failing to fully commit oneself to the mission of the local church causes an equally catastrophic rip in an individual's life. There is but one mission for the sake of Christ in this world, and everyone must find his or her own unique expression of it. Every pastor and leader must help others in the congregation in that search. Some are called to the poor and homeless. Some are called to minister to families with young children. Some are called to young adults. There are countless expressions, and church leaders are key to the fulfillment of that expression in the congregation as a whole. Someone who serves a church and does not absolutely believe that the congregation's expression of that mission is God's work, should stop and find a new church. If we do not believe in the local church's mission, we are engaged in work that is not ours. Doing so will tear the fabric of our own identities. If it is ours (and I find it often is), then we must find a way to commit our whole selves to it.

Generosity to the Local Church beyond General Giving

I pray no one reads arrogance in my call for greater and more widespread generosity. I've failed often. Still, I want to go a step further. Pastors and church leaders must also be prepared to be generous with the local church in ways beyond the tithe. I can think of at least three: fundraisers, capital campaigns, and miscellaneous opportunities.

First, my Southern Baptist heritage (I became a United Methodist at age twenty) nearly prevents me from saying this, but pastors must be generous with the local church in various fundraising endeavors. Southern Baptists and other evangelical traditions may simply disallow fundraising. They make the compelling argument that if a local church is called to a particular ministry, then it ought to be supported by the tithes and offerings (mostly tithes) of the church members. Like it or not, that's pretty compelling.

United Methodist congregations just don't see it this way. The youth hold a pumpkin patch to support a mission trip. The women sell cookies for the missions of the General Board of Global Ministries. The men host a turkey shoot for a local feeding ministry. The choir holds a spaghetti dinner to purchase new robes. A new church start has a trivia night just trying to get itself off the ground. If it has potential to raise money for ministry, United Methodists have probably tried it; maybe not bingo, raffles, or beer gardens, but nothing would surprise me. And, I've been invited to every sort of fundraiser just named, though the turkey shoot wasn't from a congregation I was serving.

I admit. I've often failed in this. I was shaped by evangelical convictions about fundraising. Local congregations should simply support the mission of their local church with tithes and offerings. But, too many times I've been wrong in how I handled situations— wrong in my idealism, wrong in the lack of grace I've offered committed members engaged in fundraising, wrong in my thinking. Fundraisers are part of the shared life in many local churches, and present opportunities to engage people in meaningful relationships, to exercise more generosity.

If leaders are to remain trusted, they must participate. They might voice concern over the theology and practicalities, but in the midst of an event, the people running the fundraisers believe they are fulfilling the greater mission of the local church. They believe they are doing something significant. Failing to participate may be received as an egregious insult.

A leader who refuses should examine his or her motivations. In the midst of my own refusals, I often found myself, in the quiet of my office or on the drive home, fuming. "I give more than 10 percent. I have a kid in daycare! Those people just don't understand! This is just one more expense I don't need!" In hindsight, I admit that my refusal was less about the purity of my convictions and more about fear and greed.

The pastor and key lay leaders need to participate, finding a way to be generous, bantering with those running events, bragging on the work, allowing the event to foster good relationships with people who make the rest of the church's ministry happen in the future. At some point, leading a congregation requires one to face conflict and keep convictions, but there are better and worse times for that. As surely as people will remember your hospital visits, sermons, and kind words in passing, they will remember the second-hand lamp you bought, the spaghetti dinner you attended, and the exuberance with which you gave.

Next, a congregation with any vitality, especially one that grows, will at some point have to find a way to pay for renovations or construction of new space, turning to some form of *capital campaign.* If you aren't already familiar, a capital campaign is an organized effort, with programmatic themes, intended to raise money outside the ordinary course of life and budget of a local church, usually with a specific project in mind. For churches with annual budgets of more than $500,000, hiring a consultant for such an event is absolutely necessary. For smaller churches unable to afford the fees of a consultant, capital campaigns can be conducted successfully, but only with mentoring of pastor and leaders by others who have successfully completed campaigns in other settings.

Capital campaigns represent important opportunities for a pastor to be generous outside of his or her tithe. In fact, they will only succeed if led by a pastor excited not just about the targeted project but about the chance to be generous during the campaign.

As with fundraisers, pastors must look at capital campaign pledges as a chance to (a) share in common work with the people they seek to lead; and (b) expand their own ability to be generous, further dropping walls that divide them from God's work.

Third, I want to offer encouragement for miscellaneous forms of generosity. There are countless opportunities to show generosity in a local church, ways that have little to do with the budget or organized fundraisers. My own life was changed for the better by a pastor who did this.

I was in my twenties, and I wasn't sure Church was really for me anymore. Still, I'd been attending a United Methodist church. Every Sunday, as is common, the church held a "donut hour" between services. The donuts were put out on a table in boxes with large coffee carafes. Baskets were placed on the table for donations. I'm not suggesting this is a great form of hospitality, but once, I remember chatting with the pastor while walking into donut hour. I was twenty-one years old and never had cash. I typically passed on the donuts, only ever opting for coffee, coffee that never seemed good enough to justify payment. On this Sunday, I walked through the line with the pastor. He told me to grab a donut. As I started to refuse, I saw him get his wallet and casually toss a twenty-dollar bill in the basket.

He never said a word. He didn't think about it. He simply gave twenty dollars for a couple donuts and bad coffee. This wasn't really the central event that drew me into The United Methodist Church, but it had an impact. He was so casual in giving twenty dollars for bad coffee and donuts, that I found myself wanting to be more giving.

In these little events, all church leaders, clergy and lay, might have the same sort of impact. All it takes is carrying a little cash or a checkbook and simply learning to give without thinking too much. My pastor had simply been shaped to give without thought; to give without concern. He did it with the twenty dollars. He did it with just about anyone who approached with a legitimate need. It was his most endearing trait. He truly was generous, and generosity is a primary building block for quality and trusted leadership.

Generosity in the Organizations of a Local Community

The work of the Church must always move from the inside out. Those of us in leadership know this. We say, "Churches must be outwardly focused." We say, "Jesus commissioned disciples to go, to move toward those who need the gospel." We say, "Christians must be mindful of reaching new generations." We know the work of the Church must always move from the inside out. We just aren't always good at doing it.

Sadly, many pastors spend little time involved in the work of communities beyond the local church. Worse, United Methodists as a denomination spend little time reflecting on cultural works that originate outside the Church, while hoping to create something compelling to those steeped in the cultural work we spend so little time considering.

I state all of this, just to make the point: church leaders must be prepared to enter and operate in a world that appears entirely secular, sometimes even hostile to the work of the Church. Good ministry requires us to be "vile," and our generosity can't be confined to the local church.

As our leadership in the local church depends on our ability to be generous with the people and ministries, so our ability to lead in the greater community depends on generosity expressed to that community. I don't mean to suggest that generosity in the outside community ought to be thought of as a means to an end. We don't express generosity to the greater community in order to Christianize the masses, though without it, we will never make such inroads. Rather, it seems to me that the call of all Christians, the commission of disciples, is to live in the world, living out the self-sacrifice modeled by Christ, not just to our local congregations, but to everyone, regardless of who they might be. If the mark of a Christian life is selfless love, that mark ought to be apparent to any and everyone we meet.

This is consistent with the Great Commission in the final chapter of the Gospel of Matthew. The translation "Go, make disciples of all the nations" misses the actual tense of the verb "to go." In a more recent translation, Jesus's words are, "As you go, make disciples of all nations." He simply assumed that disciples would be living and working among others, and that as part of their lives, moving among other people, some even hostile to the faith, they were/are to share the faith through generosity and self-giving.

My critique of so many pastors isn't meant to suggest this never happens. Many actually do this in remarkable ways. When a tornado destroyed part of Joplin, Missouri, in 2011, the United Methodist pastors there became critical leaders in the community, supporting a host of organizations and work. I also remember a fundraising dinner of a community organization serving homeless women. A retired pastor I consider a mentor and friend shocked me by leading the giving for the evening, announcing a large personal gift. I admit to feeling shame in my own offering that night.

15

Incredible things begin to happen when we don't restrain our generosity. "Secular" organizations may develop interests in partnerships, providing new opportunities for ministry. Generous Christians make the Church what it was always supposed to be, a gathering of people who lead the world in love.

If we imagine our role in terms of presenting the life of Christ in all we do, there is no better opportunity than to give generously to efforts beyond the local church. Here, we will have a chance not to draw attention to ourselves so much as to draw attention to the generosity that should always characterize the Church. When we give beyond our local church's ministry, we present Christian love in a wider circle. Our generosity becomes part of our proclamation.

Generosity Day In and Day Out

This representation of Christ and the Church goes beyond giving financial gifts to outside organizations. Those of us who live and work in small towns are especially aware of the incredible number of opportunities to be generous.

A couple times a year, walking into the grocery store can be a risky endeavor. The Girl Scouts and Boy Scouts will be peddling their cookies or popcorn. When entering the store, when the scouts approach, the extra calories notwithstanding, we should go ahead and order. That's sometimes hard for me to say. The Boy Scouts and Girl Scouts represent enormous numbers of children. No matter what one might think about the organizations, the sales of cookies for Girl Scouts and popcorn for Boy Scouts represent activities of children who believe they are doing good work. A simple "yes" and ten dollars may build the confidence of a child. "No" risks casting you and the Church as closed and irrelevant. Given that generosity and open postures should always characterize our lives, a few purchases are simply part of leadership.

On behalf of the Muscular Dystrophy Association, firefighters brave the busiest intersections, and like those in the local church running the rummage sale, the men and women passing the boot to drivers believe they are engaged in important work for people with Muscular Dystrophy. Always in the name of generosity, spare change in the boot represents affirmation, encouragement, and Christian love.

Church leaders ought to frequent school barbecues, band or color guard car washes, and even Lenten fish fries at the Catholic Church. Why? Not only do they put us among real people who deserve our generosity, but they force us to let go of selfish interests. Even paying for the groceries of the woman struggling in the checkout lane can become a demonstration of healthy generosity.

II. A Theological Approach to Generosity

The Lord said to Cain, "Why are you angry, and why do you look so resentful? If you do the right thing, won't you be accepted? But if you don't do the right thing, sin will be waiting at the door ready to strike! It will entice you, but you must rule over it."

—Genesis 4:6-7

My favorite Bible story about generosity is not one that most think of as a story about generosity. Most people understand the story of Cain and Abel in terms of murder, jealousy, and fratricide (brother killing brother). But, I think it's a story about human posture with respect to God, creation, and others.

Taking the passage as it appears (Gen 4:1-16), Cain, a crop farmer, and his brother, Abel, a shepherd, start by doing exactly as they were supposed to. They raised their crops and livestock, setting aside a portion of the produce as an offering to the Lord. In the ancient world, that meant ritually burning the offering. For reasons that aren't explained, God, observing the offering, had regard for Abel's, but not Cain's.

Cain resented God's regard for his brother's offering, grew angry, and apparently, looked the part. God observed Cain's anger and directly asked why he was mad. The text doesn't provide a response from Cain. God simply warned that if Cain allowed himself to be resentful and angry, his emotions would seize control of him, devouring him like an animal, metaphorically suggesting that Cain risked being consumed. Cain didn't heed the warning, and invited his brother to the fields where he rose up and murdered him. From there, the exchange between God and Cain is even more well-known, but Cain's act and fate were already sealed.

We can read the story many ways, but the focus on Cain's response to God's regard for Abel's offering is of particular interest. Old Testament scholar Walter Brueggeman suggested that the story metaphorically presents two particularly human problems: the *problem of God* and the *problem of other people*.[3] The *problem of God* isn't so much a problem as it is an issue with the human condition. We live in a world created by God, but which is often inherently unfair. Every human being has experienced the unfairness of creation. The *problem of other people* arises when others, especially

---

3. Walter Brueggeman, *Genesis: A Bible Commentary for Teaching and Preaching* (Atlanta: John Knox, 1982), 54–63.

those close to us, succeed while we fail. Both problems pose the risk of resentment, and here the author(s) of Genesis provide an apt metaphor. Left unaddressed, resentment does, in fact, devour people, consuming lives, negatively directing behaviors. Resentment consumed Cain and he acted accordingly.

Perhaps we might object, insisting that no matter how resentful, one doesn't have to commit murder. But this needs to be considered carefully. From the start, the story offers a hint of its direction, at least for those who know Hebrew or read footnotes. In every Bible I checked, the name *Abel* is footnoted with the meaning of the name—"nothingness." Cain resents Abel, falling prey to the beast of his emotions, allowing it to consume his behaviors, robbing him of the ability to see the humanity of his brother, moving him to conduct in material terms what he had already done emotionally and spiritually, eliminating Abel's existence. Resentment robs us of the ability to see humanity in others, driving us inward. We may not physically commit murder, but when we resent others, we do what Cain did. We blind ourselves. We render people as *nothing*.

Of course, there's hope. God is clear in Genesis: if we work at it, we can "master" or "rule over" our resentment. We have the power to take control of our lives, to turn away from self toward a full acknowledgment of others.

This is the very essence of generosity, turning from self to the other. As Christians, we must master our tendency to turn away from others and toward self. Here's the hard lesson of Cain and Abel: We have two choices. We may choose to be generous, acknowledging the humanity of others, extending ourselves in giving and relationship. Or, we can refuse, allowing our tendency toward resentment, failing to face the problems inherent in living in the created world with other people, blinding ourselves to the humanity of others, shutting ourselves off, emotionally and spiritually eliminating the existence of other people.

We only make the turn to others through an intentional effort. It takes effort to become generous, starting rather than finishing with the giving of our financial resources, reflecting on those gifts in ways that shape who we are as people, using that reflection as a springboard to greater growth, opening ourselves to be consumed by the idea that we can give our whole self for other people. In other words, by exploring all four types of financial giving laid out in this chapter, a pastor and/or church leader may be shaped in positive ways emotionally, intellectually, and spiritually.

We might start by trying our hands at all four types of generosity. We can start small, making a commitment to tithe. We might just carry some cash and a check so that it's easy to drop money into church fundraising events. We can call the local school district and ask what the principal or PTO president might do with a $500 or $1,000 gift. If that's too much, we can call and offer $100 to be used however the PTO thinks best. We can allow ourselves to say yes to the Girl Scouts during cookie season, the postal workers during their food drive, and the bell ringers at Christmas. We only need to make an effort. Then, each time we make a contribution, no matter how big or small, we should reflect and pray on it. If it was a struggle, we should ask, what was lost by giving? If anything was lost at all, was it that important? What might we have gained? What good might come of it? Theologically, what might God do with the money we gave? Pray. Pray that God might through our giving bring about some small transformation of the world for the better. Pray that God might transform us through the act of giving.

The story of Cain and Abel presents us with two ways of living in the world. We either allow ourselves to be consumed with our own resentments, closing ourselves, eliminating our awareness of others, or we face the world with a posture of generosity. That's really the crux of what I'm suggesting in the first chapter. All finance and administration must be backed up by a posture of generosity, of openness.

The church treasurer who refuses to see anything other than the need to build the church's reserves has missed the point. He or she has faced the job with a closed posture, one shaped more by anxiety, fear, and resentment, than generosity. Pastors do the same thing when they try to use church finances to shape their own agendas, failing to incorporate laity into a conversation about the direction of the church. I'm an advocate for strong central leadership of churches. But, even the best pastors must have a group of strong, generous laity, who help shape direction. Pastors who rule with iron fists do so out of insecurity or resentment or anger, and it never goes well. Leadership must always be generous, the activities conducted only to benefit the local church and its community.

Imagine a church treasurer who, when sitting down to look at the financial reports, first prays, "God, help me to see in these numbers the possibility for more generosity, more good in the surrounding community, more transformation for the good of the people who might attend this church. Amen." Suddenly, the financial reports become means of evaluating programs that benefit the church and the people in town. They become tools demonstrating the health of the individuals who lead and attend the local church. They become a means of spotting more ways the church might make an impact. The first priority of the church should be a positive impact on the world around its attendees. Imagine a pastor who is always generous with the congregation and local community. Imagine the credibility that's built, how such credibility and generosity would change people for the better. I don't mean just financial generosity. Instead, imagine a pastor who has allowed generosity and an open posture to shape his or her entire ministry. Learning to graciously say no to certain activities and gifts will be critical to the pastor's health. But, starting from a posture of openness, as Bishop Schnase would describe it, with a willingness to say yes, can only ever be a means of leading with power, authority, and credibility.

This is where financial and administrative leadership begins: with a posture of openness, such posture shaped by giving, but also trust in God, in others and in the good creation God has given. This posture of giving and trust will be the recurring theme in every item explored in this book. When in doubt about what steps to take in leadership, giving and trust will always provide helpful criteria.

Personal Budgets: Planning for God's Work in Life

Christians must always face life with an open posture, giving, turning to others, staying vigilant to what God might have them do. An open posture carries a willingness to change directions when needed, but lives lived well also require intentionality.

A comparison might be drawn to worship planning. The best services, regardless of denominational tradition or style, are at once flexible, open to the movement of the Spirit, and intentionally well planned. Don Saliers, my worship professor at Emory University, always said, "The Holy Spirit never precludes good planning." The same goes for our individual lives, especially our personal finances.

Finances must be approached with good planning, individually and organizationally, even as we remain open to changing plans. *Budgets* are financial plans. I'll address organizational budgets in part II, but leaders must begin with personal budgets, ensuring they have the integrity needed to lead others. Here, I will lay out one process for constructing a personal budget—one with theological underpinnings and that begins with the priority for generosity. You may have your own process. Whatever it is, my prayer is that you develop a good plan, one that allows you to flourish in ministry. I haven't known many people who enjoy budgeting. To many, the thought of curbing desired spending is truly a vile practice. Still, budgets keep us on track for fruitful ministry.

I. Practices and Patterns of Personal Budgeting

A budget is a plan, a road map, or a blueprint. Before creating a budget, one must begin by deciding what they want the results of that plan to be. For many, personal budgeting is a plan for building wealth. For the Christian, I think the purpose should be different.

When it comes to organizations, a budget should always reflect the greater purpose and values of that organization. This is no less true for individuals and families. A household's budget should reflect the greater purpose and values of the individual or family creating it. Instead of building wealth, Christians should think in terms similar to those we used in chapter 1. We may dread thinking about all we may not be able to spend, but submitting to a budget can be a means to discerning and focusing on our ministries.

We might think of our Christian purpose in many different ways. We might imagine it in terms of making ourselves more open to God's purpose, more open to being generous, more open to the unique thing we and our family members were made to do. Readers should spend some time discussing the way their families articulate their greater purposes before starting the process of building a budget. Doing so will highlight the values and activities the budget is meant to support.

No matter how an individual's purpose is articulated, we can describe a general approach to budgeting. Creating a budget requires four basic steps: (1) accounting for and counting God-given resources; (2) accounting for the need to be generous; (3) counting the costs needed to support our household in its ultimate purposes; and (4) tracking our resources and spending, while evaluating our need to make changes.

Counting Resources as God's Gifts

"Counting resources" means counting the money that you anticipate will come into your household. You might expand this practice to include any resources you can name. For example, if someone in your household anticipates finishing some form of education that will lead to an increase in pay, you should name that and account for the way it will affect your income. This is a simple process, though it may be far from easy. Counting resources involves thoughtfully writing them down, spending time carefully thinking about each one. If the resource is clearly financial, write the amount anticipated for the entire year.

Starting in the middle of a calendar year is okay. This just requires us to look ahead and complete the process again in December for the full following year.

Imagine Jack, a nurse, who's married to Sally, a United Methodist pastor. We can develop their family's budget and the details needed to do so over the course of the next few pages. Their counting of resources might include Jack's wages, Sally's salary and housing allowance, some small returns from an investment account, and gifts. Suppose Jack, who receives hourly pay, anticipates $53,000 in the coming year. Sally serves a congregation in Kansas City, receiving a salary of $45,000 and a combined housing and utilities allowance of $18,000 a year. Their other income typically includes a gift from Sally's well-to-do parents at Christmas of about $5,000, a gift they've always received. And, Jack began investing a small amount of the family's savings a few years ago, almost as a hobby. He anticipates returns from dividends and capital gains from that investment account to be around $500 this year. As such, their list would include the following:

Jack's Salary	$53,000	$4,417/month
Sally's Salary	$45,000	$3,750/month
Sally's Housing	$18,000	$1,500/month
Gift	$5,000	
Investment Gains	$500	
Total	**$121,500**	**$10,125/month**

When the individual or family pairs the practice of listing with a clear expression of thanksgiving, it becomes a healthy spiritual practice. Jack and Sally might sit down and make the list together, offering a short prayer of thanksgiving for each. Understanding their income in terms of a gift, in terms of resources given to complete the work God has called them to do, will establish a healthy approach to money that begins with openness rather than greed.

Once resources are listed, the next step requires naming costs associated with expressions of generosity.

Counting the Costs of Generosity

Ministry, like grace, is never cheap. We all know that. Those of us who are pastors yielded our entire lives, including the lives of our families, to do the work we believe God made us to do. Lay leaders have no less of a call on their own lives, and those who find their way to the strongest, deepest levels of commitment are just as aware of the cost of doing God's work. Our vocations, ordained or lay, cost something. As those vocations evolve, so will the costs. At the very least, we must account for the costs of generosity in the local church and community, as well as costs associated with taking deeper steps into ministry.

Let's return to Jack and Sally's budget. As with any Christian's list of costs, Jack and Sally should begin with their tithe to the local church Sally is serving and the rest of the family is attending. Remember, Jack makes about $53,000 a year. Sally makes $45,000 in cash plus another $18,000 in housing. They expect $5,000 in gifts and another $500 in investment returns. Add it all up. Take 10 percent. We shouldn't quibble over whether they add Sally's mileage reimbursements or returns from retirement. Readers making the same list who start asking what to include or not should just make a decision. For Sally and Jack, the math adds up to $121,500. If they tithe 10 percent, their pledge to the local church is $12,150 or $1,012.50 a month.

In addition, last year, the church held a capital campaign to renovate the sanctuary. Sally and Jack did as the consultant suggested and made a significant commitment of $12,000 to the campaign. The campaign is a three-year program currently in the second year. For the coming year, Sally and Jack will be giving $4,000 over their tithe, or about $334 a month.

Finally, they also decided to find ways to be generous in town. Because they are giving in generous ways for the church, especially with the capital campaign, suppose they start small, suppose they set aside $100 a month that either of them can give to fundraisers or other charitable purposes.

Sally and Jack have largely settled into their careers and have no educational aspirations. As such, their accounting of the costs for their own ministry can stop here, so long as they remember that all of life might be thought of as ministry. These costs, therefore, take priority over any they might incur. In a sense, their whole budget is meant to fund and fuel this generosity, to fund and fuel their lives in ministry. Everything else in the budget is, therefore, the cost of doing business as ministers.

Sally and Jack, generous by most accounts, still have more than 85 percent of their income (more than $100,000), just to run their household.

$121,500 of income
-$12,150 tithe
-$4,000 campaign gift
-$1,200 general
= $104,150 left to run the household

Each year, they should move increasing amounts of their income into the costs of generosity. They may never get to 100 percent unless by some miracle the government stops collecting taxes, they find ways to eat on the generosity of others, and they find they have plenty banked for retirement. Still, it's amazing how people find ways to become more generous.

Counting the Costs of the Household

Now, the hard work really begins. At this point, we must account for the rest of the household's costs. I can almost guarantee, once one starts listing, there will be more costs than anticipated and more spending than needed. People tend to optimistically assume they won't spend as much as they will really need for certain essential items. We tend to look on the bright side, hoping for more of the things we don't need, failing to recognize the full cost of what we do. Sorting through a list of expenses is incredibly healthy because it forces us to reflect on what we really need to do the work to which God calls us, and just how much we waste on nonessential items.

We should start with debt. With many other Christian financial advisers, I strongly urge against carrying debt, especially from consumer goods. No matter how commonly such advice is given, I continue to talk to individuals who don't understand that they pay back more to a lender than the amount they borrow. *Interest* charged by lenders represents a premium paid by the borrower for the privilege of using someone else's money.

We might debate whether some debt is better than other. For example, many argue that the low interest rates on home loans and the past precedent of rising real-estate prices means that borrowing to buy a new home allows individuals to make a good investment they wouldn't otherwise be able to make. Similar arguments are made for student loans.

These loans also tend to be made at lower interest rates, with interest on some loans waived while the borrower is in school. Student loans allow people who couldn't otherwise afford it to obtain an education, establishing them with better earning power for the rest of their lives. Interest paid on education debt and home loans is even deductible from federal income tax. At the same time, no one should misunderstand. *All* loans carry interest and fees. Individuals pay more to the lender than they would if they used their own funds. No one who can afford a home or an education without a loan should incur the debt if they don't have to. Too much debt can be devastating to a person's financial health, regardless of advantages.

While small student loans and a reasonable home loan might be beneficial, consumer debt seldom is. I understand that, at times, an individual might need a loan to buy a car or some other item. However, debt incurred for *consumer goods* should be avoided if at all possible. The interest, especially on credit cards, is usually higher, meaning that it takes more money to pay back the loan. Second, there is no tax advantage, and the items purchased with consumer debt, unlike homes or student loans, have almost no chance of increasing in value. Cars depreciate the moment we drive them home from the dealer. Other consumer goods are, as the classification suggests, *consumed* in short order.

All the negative associations with debt in mind, my advice is the same as that of other writers and teachers on the subject: eliminate as much debt as you can, as quickly as you can. Thus, current debt becomes a priority among the costs of running your household. Except in rare circumstances, I highly suggest paying more than the amount you owe the lender each month. The more quickly you pay down debt, the less interest you'll be obligated to pay.

On the list of expenses, we start with each and every loan we owe, calculating the monthly payment, adding any extra we can afford, and writing it down on our list. If we find we have more money than we thought at the end of the process, these payments might be a good place to return, adding any extra that's possible. Always pay extra toward the debt with the highest interest rates first. This will allow for the most savings.

Once we've dealt with debt, we move on to taxes, especially those that would ordinarily be deducted from a paycheck. Taxes are a certainty. We are obligated to pay them, and for clergy, the situation is complicated by the fact that we pay self-employment tax, rather than FICA, which would be deducted from a paycheck. Clergy must be astute enough to estimate their federal and state taxes, and to budget for them each month, having the employer deduct additional amounts from a paycheck or setting enough aside for quarterly IRS payments. This maximizes the need to place the expenses associated with these taxes early in our budgets.

From here, we have a bit more flexibility. We must establish priorities for expenses. We may have to estimate costs based on past experiences. We can tweak this over time, but must be as honest and realistic as possible. We should try to account for every household expense, including all utilities, groceries, clothing, auto insurance, gasoline, cell phones, medical costs, home Internet, pets, childcare, and home or garden costs. In some of these items, we find flexibility to save and add to other items. In others, we may have to spend more than we thought.

We must not neglect emergency, college, and retirement savings. I'll visit the different sorts of pension programs, especially those available to United Methodist clergy, in the next chapter, but both businesses and churches have moved to plans requiring individuals to set aside their own amounts for their own retirement. Social Security will simply not be enough for most people. I'm not a financial advisor, but the more we can set aside, the better. If we can only start with 2 or 3 percent of income, that's okay; but we should work to grow beyond 10 percent, especially as we reduce debt. Families with children may also want to think about setting aside for college savings.

Finally, we finish with items that are nonessential. By nonessential, I do not mean unimportant. These are just the items with which we have more flexibility. Everyone should set aside for entertainment and personal development. We might even divide that into categories like "piano lesson costs," "camp costs," "vacation savings," or "date night funds." We should budget for these because we will, if working hard in ministry, need a break. Our families will need time together, and our kids will need extracurricular opportunities.

Let's assume that Jack and Sally have two children. Their monthly expenses might look like this:

Giving/Generosity	
Tithe	-1,012.50
Capital	-333.34
Other	-100

Taxes	
Sally Fed	-525
Jack Fed	-300
Social Security/Medicare Tax	-1140
Sally State	-200
Jack State	-112
Personal Property	-78.75

Debt	
Home Loan	-1100
Car Payment	-425

Household	
Cell Phone	-200
Groceries	-750
Kids Lunch	-20
Medical	-150
Clothing	-125
Home & Garden	-250

Household	
Misc/Furnishings	-250
Water Bill	-100
Electric Bill	-100
Landline Bill/Cable/Internet	-200

Entertainment	
Entertainment	-250
Travel	-200

Extracurricular	
Piano Lessons	-45
Soccer Registration	-55
Swimming Lessons	-12

Automotive	
Gas	-375
Insurance	-145
Maintenance	-100

Insurance	
Sally Life Insurance	-18
Jack Life Insurance	-33
Kids Life Insurance	-30
Jack/Kids Health Insurance	-175

Savings	
Sally PIP	-400
Jack 401 (k)	-450
General	-50
College Savings	-250

Assemble the Plan

All that's left is to assemble the budget. Split all of the income into monthly amounts and add them together. This is our budgeted monthly income. Next, assemble the monthly costs of generosity and add them to the monthly costs associated with debt and the household expenses. Remember, we haven't actually incurred the expenses or received the income yet. *This is a plan.* We subtract the expected and estimated expenses from expected and estimated income. If the amount remaining is negative, we must go back and find ways to increase income or reduce expenses. Ways to increase income might be adding additional employment or finding ways to reliably increase returns on an investment. Keep in mind that no income is ever certain. We must be reasonable in what we plan. Reducing expenses may necessitate reducing the amount budgeted for entertainment. Check on hard-to-estimate items like groceries or the electric bill.

If the amount left is positive, we're headed in the right direction. We may want to live into the plan for a few months to make sure we haven't underestimated certain expenses. But, once you are certain you are making more than you're spending, you may want to go back and increase your debt reduction or retirement savings. We might also increase generosity. But, unless we have kept the entertainment budget too low, I wouldn't encourage using extra to purchase more consumer or nonessential items.

Remember, the whole idea is to pay for our ministry. This means that our generosity, debt reduction, and saving for future ministry should always remain our highest priority.

For a sample budget, see www.nateberneking.com.

Implementing the Plan

Implementation might be the hardest part of budgeting. Implementing the plan requires a combination of tracking actual income and what we actually spend, holding ourselves accountable to the plan. If we planned $200 for entertainment, then $200 is the limit. If we planned an extra $100 a month on a student loan, then we must actually pay the extra $100. We must actually contribute the tithe to the church or the gift to the capital campaign. Implementing the plan is complicated because real life can make things difficult. Cars break down. Kids get sick and need a doctor. We might even find ourselves with a speeding ticket or, worse, a car accident.

The budget, as a plan, may need to change, but holding ourselves accountable requires effort. The budget forces us to reflect on what we're spending and where. In so doing, it is a constant reminder of priorities and plans for carrying out our own vocations.

II. A Theological Approach to Personal Budgets

Happy are you who are poor, because God's kingdom is yours. . . . But how terrible for you who are rich, because you have already received your comfort.

—Luke 6:20, 24

We need to be honest. As easy as it is to theologically support generosity, other financial practices are harder to justify, having their roots in a system that is explicitly secular, one that names the expansion of wealth as the primary goal. In later chapters, we'll see that Jesus had something to say about that. Yet, this doesn't mean that all financial and administrative practices must be abandoned. In fact, the basis for many of those practices is to hold the practitioner accountable to their stated goal. If, as Christians, we rename the stated goal in terms of God's work of redemption and sanctification in the world, we can use the same sorts of practices to hold ourselves and our churches accountable to goals that are more consistent with the words of Jesus, the teachings of the Church, the general approach to life suggested by the Scriptures.

Budgeting presents this sort of challenge. Most people assume that the practice of personal budgeting has as its aim the growth of wealth. Create a budget, stick to it, hold yourself accountable, and ensure that you are saving and investing to maximize income and grow wealth. If, however, we have named some goal in terms of God's redemption of a broken world, and we prioritize generosity and openness, then budgeting practices can be used to hold ourselves accountable to something more divine.

The theological basis for this sort of accountability must start with an assessment of the human condition. Another teacher of mine, Luke Timothy Johnson, produced a seminal work on possessions.[1] In it, he examines the way Jesus dealt with possessions in the Gospel of Luke. According to Johnson, the problems of possessions begin with the human tendency toward idolatry. At our most basic level, we are all idolaters.

By idolatry, Johnson means that human beings tend to place ultimate significance in just about everything other than a transcendent God. At the center of our lives, we place our families, our jobs, our friends, and maybe most significantly, our possessions, using one or more of these finite features of life as the key motivation for behavior. Johnson paints a compelling view of how this

---

1. Luke Timothy Johnson, *Sharing Possessions: What Faith Demands,* 2nd ed. (Grand Rapids: Eerdmans, 2011).

happens. We tend to infuse our own identity in these things. We treat them as extensions of ourselves.[2] As a result, when someone insults our family or friends, we feel insulted. In a more widespread feeling, when someone has stolen something from us or broken into our homes, we feel "violated." Why? Our friends, loved ones, and possessions become extensions of ourselves.

I, like Johnson, don't condemn anyone for feeling these things. We all experience them because they are part of existence. Jesus seemed to understand this. All of his teachings in the Gospel of Luke suggest that we must always check our tendency to align ourselves with our possessions. He said, "Happy are you who are poor, for God's kingdom is yours," contrasting it with "But how terrible for you who are rich, because you have already received your comfort" (Luke 6:20, 24). A rich person attempts to find comfort in wealth, while the poor have nowhere to turn but to something transcendent in hope of better times. The story of the "rich young ruler" in Luke 18 illustrates this. A rich man asks Jesus what he must do to inherit eternal life. Jesus tells him to follow the commandments, but the man is insistent that he's already been doing that. Jesus responds with his infamous response, "There's one more thing. Sell everything you own and distribute the money to the poor. Then . . . come, follow me" (v. 22). The young man simply walked away downcast, for "he was extremely rich" (v. 23). Jesus looked straight to the heart of the matter, pointing out that the man was blocked from experiencing the fullness of life by his own preoccupation with possessions. When told to give them all away, he showed this to be true.

We are natural idolaters, and like the rich young man, we are hopeful that God would never ask us to give up our possessions. Regardless of what God might require, we're often blocked by the

2. Ibid., 39–50.

distraction our wealth and possessions create. We are hesitant to trust in God enough to even entertain a willingness to yield our possessions to someone else.

Should we run out and give all we own to the poor? I suppose that depends. Undoubtedly, we must constantly curb the tendency to place our identity in wealth. We need systems of accountability to ensure that we are at least moving toward the sort of openness and trust that Jesus suggested as the key to "eternal life" and the "kingdom of God." It is in this openness and trust that we come to know what transcendence really is, what God really is.

If we shift priorities and values in our personal budgets from maximizing wealth to equipping ourselves to do what we believe God made us to do, then those budgets can become powerful tools needed to build lives characterized by generosity.

As natural idolaters, holding God at the center of life, following even the first of the commandments, requires us to make conscious and intentional efforts to prioritize our lives in healthy ways. Put another way, we need a plan for life. Like pilgrims traveling closer to a location they know as a center of spiritual meaning, we require a plan, a map, that leads us down a path of becoming progressively most trusting, more open. We need something against which we can constantly measure ourselves and the journey we've made. This is why I intentionally stated that budgets must always be understood in terms of plans.

How we live is the evidence of the people we have become. How we spend is an expression of our identity, our values, our priorities. When that spending is associated with an effort to be increasingly generous to do ministry, we begin to approach the lives God created for us in the first place. Budgets can and should be expressions of the sort of spending we associate with generosity and openness.

Chapter 3

Retirement Savings: Preparing for God's Work after a Paycheck

Each chapter now builds. In chapter 1, we laid some ground-work. Financial and administrative leadership must begin with generosity. In chapter 2, we explored budgeting associated with a posture of generosity. Now, let's consider more deeply one part of the planning involved with budgeting—retirement savings.

Unfortunately, many pastors have little understanding of how they will fund retirement. Most understand that the denomination maintains a pension plan, but remain unaware of details. They have even less knowledge of other sorts of income they will have in retirement or how to set money aside. Most, the young especially, simply prefer not to think about it. Regardless of the reasons, people often prefer not to think about it, what they might need, from where it will come.

Not thinking about it sets up a difficult future. Most employer-provided plans like the United Methodist pension won't be suffi-cient. For pastors who serve churches for thirty-five or forty years, a monthly retirement check may come, but most will find the amount less than sufficient to accomplish whatever it is they desire. It will, at least, be much less than the salary they were accustomed to receiving. Like most plans, the United Methodist pension plan assumes that participants will engage in their own savings and rely on assistance from the government in the form of Social Security. Whether lay or clergy, if we do not understand what our retirement will be like, if we do not at least spend time thinking about it, including the sort of ministry we might seek to fulfill after retirement, we will have no idea what we must do in the present in order to prepare. Most of us will want our ministries to continue in some form, even if that only means attending a local church and supporting its ministries.

In this chapter, I won't give any particular investment advice. Instead, I plan on defining some terms and explaining the basics of pension plans, using the United Methodist plan as the central illustration. United Methodist clergy and laity will find this particularly helpful, but even clergy and leaders from other denominations will be able to read this as a basic primer into various types of retirement plans and savings vehicles. True to the pattern we set in chapter 1, the chapter will end with a theological justification for retirement savings. As you'll see, we can only justify retirement savings if we understand that we are only setting wealth aside for the purpose of preparing for ministry following receipt of a last paycheck.

I. Practices and Patterns of Individual Retirement Savings

I want to describe several types of retirement savings. I'll divide the discussion into two parts. First, I'll describe various *employer-*

provided pension or savings programs with special emphasis given to those provided by The United Methodist Church. Then, I'll offer a brief look at a few savings vehicles available to the *general public*. I'm not a financial planner. There are publications with much more information than what I can offer. And, I encourage those with the capacity, to locate a professional who can help develop a strategy for saving and investing.

Employer Plans

I've probably already established some confusion, using the words *pension plans* ambiguously. For many, a *pension* has a more specific meaning and can be contrasted with *savings plans*. That said, employers, specifically large denominations, might offer both. Even small employers may offer versions of savings plans, though those more closely resemble the sort of accounts the general public will utilize. Most employees in large mainstream denominations, and all pastors (at least those working more than in very part-time capacities) in The United Methodist Church, have access to one of the following sorts of plans.

(1) Defined Benefit Plans

Often, the word *pension* is used to describe a *defined benefit plan*. In these, employers contribute to a pooled and invested fund on behalf of employees. At times, the contribution, or part of it, is actually deducted from the employee's paycheck. When the employee retires, the plan sends regular payments based on some formula, to the retired employee. The benefit from the plan is established or *defined* and will continue regardless of circumstances until the retiree dies (and occasionally until the retiree and his or her spouse dies). In order to obtain the benefit, for it to *vest*, employees sometimes must provide long-time service to the employer, say at least twenty years. The amount of the benefit might also be increased for each year an employee worked.

In concrete terms, an employee works a career for the employer, during which the employer sets aside money into a pension fund. After thirty years, the employee retires. As soon as retirement takes effect, a regular check will begin to be sent.

For much of the middle twentieth century, this is how employees planned for retirement. They worked long careers, having contributions made on their behalf. Most of America's large companies, local governments, and school districts used this sort of plan. From the perspective of retirees, the system is wonderful, especially following the creation of Social Security. Many retirees receive two regular monthly checks. With these plans, employees don't have to think much about retirement. They are simply provided for by their former employer and the US government.

From the employer's perspective, defined benefit plans present a challenge. When done well and administered conservatively, these plans still provide a significant benefit for retirees who were highly valued by their employers, but they also have many critics. The truth is, the way they were administered and funded in many settings created enormous problems. Problems arise for the employer when more employees begin to retire and take advantage of the benefit. The problems are magnified when those same retirees begin to live longer lives. That's especially true when retirees begin living more years after retirement than the number of years they worked. When that happens, the amounts paid out during retirement will be much more than the employee had contributed.

When these plans were developed, employers understood this would be an issue. To compensate for the fact that some retirees would live more years than they actually worked, employers relied on (a) some employees living shorter lives; and (b) returns from investments made with the money in the pension fund. Problems developed in the late twentieth century when life expectancy began to increase and especially, when world markets suffered significant setbacks in 1989, 2000, and 2008. In those setbacks, pension funds lost value, meaning that they didn't have enough to pay the benefits to all of the current and projected retirees. Plan administrators and actuaries have a phrase to describe the problem: *unfunded liabilities*, obligations for which there are no funds. The plan will be liable to retirees for benefit payments, but those payments have insufficient funding.

To complicate the situation, the cost of living rose rather significantly in the United States over the last half century. For retirees with "fixed incomes," this meant that they needed more money in retirement. They could not count on normal raises like the workforce. Instead, they had to demand more benefits. This put pressure on the pension plans to increase funding, but that meant that as more people retired, the liabilities for benefit payments increased more than anticipated. When investments dropped in value, employers found their unfunded liabilities more significant than they dreamed possible.

When plan administrators realized this, they took steps, some eventually making the problem even worse. Some employers began making higher contributions for current employees. This increased the cost of defined benefit plans. Worse, some began looking for ways to increase the returns on the investments made by the fund. They invested in higher-risk investments. When those paid off, the unfunded liabilities did get smaller. Unfortunately, high-risk investments stand to lose more in market failures, increasing the unfunded liability to even greater amounts, something realized in the financial crisis of 2008.

These issues caused many American businesses to entirely eliminate plans for future employees. A recent *Wall Street Journal* article noted that in the later years of the twentieth century, more than two hundred American companies used a defined benefit plan. Today, the number has been cut to fewer than forty.[1] Following the recession and stock market collapse of 2008, many local governments were forced to cut benefits for retirees or, in more dire circumstances, file for bankruptcy. Some retirees simply lost all or a portion of their pension checks.

Despite these problems, many defined benefit plans, especially in education and mainstream denominations, remain solvent and provide a great benefit for retirees. This, however, would not be the case without concessions from retirees.

The United Methodist Church has maintained a defined benefit plan since 1982. In that year, The UMC also developed a retroactively applied defined benefit plan for pastors and employees working in years before 1982. Unfortunately, the formula used to calculate the payments to those individuals created a situation in which the plan occasionally suffered unfunded liabilities. Some parts of The UMC (i.e., annual conferences) still experience unfunded liabilities, though the funding of the pre-82 plan is healthier overall. After 1982, the denomination attempted to keep a defined benefit plan, one that remained fully funded throughout the Church. Its initial effort didn't quite accomplish this, but changes

---

1. Timothy Martin, "Hedge-Fund Bet Hits Pensions," *The Wall Street Journal*, June 16, 2015.

after 2007 have come closer. Of course, the denomination, through its General Conference, later decided that the plan was still too expensive and lowered the benefit paid to retirees with years of service after 2013, a change that will bring reduced payments to clergy who begin ministry now and retire in the 2040s and '50s. Still, the denomination maintains the defined benefit.

Here's how it works today. First, local churches are required to make contributions for pastors in the plan (this varies by Conference, but often any pastor serving more than one-fourth time) in an amount equal to 9.22 percent of the pastor's compensation. Lay employees participate in a different sort of plan. The plan defines compensation in terms of cash salary plus housing allowance (or if a parsonage is provided, an additional 25 percent of the cash salary). I'd point out that 9.22 percent is fairly high, but the idea of the contribution is to ensure that the future liabilities remain fully funded. Then, the administrator, an organization called Wespath Benefits and Investments (formerly, the General Board of Pension and Health Benefits), takes those contributions and invests them in a pooled fund, allowing the investments to rise and fall over time. They anticipate, based on historical data, a projected return of about 6 percent per year. Pastors immediately vest in the plan, but will not receive a full or "normal" benefit unless they work at least thirty-five years or reach age sixty-five. The full annual benefit they receive upon retirement is based on a formula. They receive an annual amount equal to 1 percent of the "denominational average compensation" multiplied by the number of years of service the pastor worked. In 2016, the denominational average compensation was $65,217. Not knowing what the denominational average compensation will be, we can't quite say what a pastor retiring in 2040 might receive, but under the current average, a pastor with thirty-five years of service

45

under this plan would receive an annual payment of $22,825 or about $1,900 a month. Again, this is entirely imaginary because the denominational average compensation increases nearly every year, even in the midst of recessions. Absent a catastrophic depression and period of deflation, pastors retiring in the 2040s will receive a much higher pension payment that will adjust each year of retirement based on average compensation. A pastor who retires before age sixty-five or thirty-five years of service may still receive a benefit upon retirement, but that benefit will be reduced.

Readers can see that the advantage of a defined benefit plan lies in its guarantee of income for retirees. On the other hand, because of the risks associated with ensuring the full funding of those benefits, the employers or administrators of the plan must work very hard to find the future dollars needed to provide those payments.

Except in the most generous of defined benefit plans, an increasingly rare breed, the amount of income produced for retirees is far from sufficient for the typical American life. Under the current formula, even a modest income of $22,000 requires more than three decades of service, leaving recipients just a few thousand dollars above the poverty level set by the federal government. Retirees in those plans must prepare in other ways.

(2) Defined Contribution Plans

In the last two decades, employers have increasingly opted for a different form of retirement funding. Rather than providing a predetermined benefit, employers have opted to shift responsibility to individual employees. That *could* mean shifting all responsibility, simply allowing employees to contribute a portion of their paychecks to retirement savings. Other employers, however, have only partially shifted responsibility, alleviating their need to account for funding of future benefits, but still providing a contribution of employer money to the employee's retirement.

In these plans, the employer defines a *contribution* to the employee's retirement. The benefit available at retirement will be whatever a portfolio of possible investments produces over the course of an employee's career. That's a technical way of saying this: the employer will contribute something, but will not guarantee what might be available at retirement. These plans are called *defined contribution* plans, and The United Methodist Church adopted one in 2007, supplementing the defined benefit plan.

Here's how it works: Every local church with a pastor must contribute 3 percent of the pastor's compensation as a defined contribution to the pastor's pension. That 3 percent is then invested in a portfolio of funds administered by Wespath. Over time, returns and interest from those investments are rolled back into the same invested funds. Given a long career, especially when a pastor's compensation increases over the years, the contributions, coupled with the compounding returns, produce an amount from which the pastor may draw to supplement income from the defined benefit plan and social security.

To better understand how investment returns and compounding interest work, see www.nateberneking.com.

This form of retirement savings introduces some new concepts. First, in these plans, the contributions are invested on the employee's behalf in *funds*, pooled money invested in a certain way. In some plans, employees are responsible for selecting the funds in which their contributions are placed. Funds are typically described and named based on the sort of investments the funds hold. They may specialize in shares of stock of publicly traded American companies or publicly traded international companies. They may also seek only fixed income investments. Sometimes, the funds are described or named based on a sense of how much risk investments in them carry. An "aggressive" fund invests the contributions in riskier, but more rewarding investments. A "conservative" fund means that returns are likely to be much lower, but the risk of losing all value is reduced. Typically, younger employees want to select more aggressive investments because they have longer periods of time to continue contributions and make up for any losses in the value of their savings. Employees near retirement should have large sums built up such that they want more conservative funds, caring less for compounding returns and more for preserving what they already have.

Selecting funds can be intimidating for employees with little or no investment experience. For that reason, many employers, including The United Methodist Church, simplify the process by automatically investing based on employees' ages and years of service. Wespath places the contributions of younger clergy in a mix of funds that tend to be more aggressive, and the contributions of older clergy in more conservative funds. I advise most pastors to allow the experts at Wespath to do this work. That in mind, I also strongly encourage pastors and lay leaders to at least understand the basics of investing and personal savings. Having some understanding of how investments work can be extremely helpful in monitoring savings managed by someone else.

Defined contribution plans also raise the possibility of *employer matching programs*. This ties our discussion of defined contribution plans to the next section on individual savings. Desiring to shift even more responsibility to employees, many employers will only make a contribution if an employee also participates through payroll deductions. In other words, employees must contribute their own money if they are to receive the defined contribution from the employer. This is how the United Methodist plan works. Clergy have 2 percent of their compensation automatically contributed to retirement, but they only receive an additional 1 percent if they also contribute 1 percent of their compensation to the provided individual savings plan. As you can see, this begins to shift responsibility for retirement savings to individuals.

(3) Individual Savings Plans

We might envision retirement plans on a continuum of responsibility. Defined benefit plans place the primary responsibility for both saving and risk on the employer, offering employees a set and guaranteed benefit upon retirement. Defined contribution plans shift responsibility away from the employer toward the individual employee. In such plans, the employer still holds responsibility for making contributions, maybe even selecting investments on behalf of the employee, but the burden of risk lies with the employee. Such plans only guarantee that the employer will contribute to them. They do not guarantee that any funds contributed will still be available to the employee upon retirement. If markets fail and the value of the employee's fund in the defined contribution plan is reduced, only the employee is hurt.

Many employers moved the pendulum even further, making individual employees responsible for their own savings. In many individual retirement plans, the employee is required to make their own contributions. Again, plans vary, some including the employer in decisions about investments, but most savings plans place responsibility for investment, or at least selection from a menu of funds, on the employee.

Many readers will have heard of these plans by reference to applicable sections of the Internal Revenue Code, 401(k) or 403(b). In either case, the Internal Revenue Code allows employees to choose whether they pay taxes on contributions to these plans or whether the distributions following retirement will be taxed. The plan known as a 401(k) may be offered to employees by employers in general business settings. Only larger employers are typically able to create such plans, but they have proliferated in the US workforce. Teachers and religious workers have the opportunity for a similar sort of plan referred to as a 403(b) plan. From the employee's perspective, these work just like 401(k) plans.

Each month, the employee may choose to have a portion of his or her paycheck deducted and contributed by the employer to the plan. The funds within each employee's account may be invested in a designated number of funds, or in some cases, even in the individual stocks of certain companies. The process looks very much like a defined contribution plan, but with only the employee making a contribution.

The United Methodist Church has such a plan to supplement the defined benefit and defined contribution plans. We call this individual savings plan, the United Methodist Personal Investment Plan or UMPIP, and it is a 403(b) plan. In the case of United Methodists investing in UMPIP, funds are placed in accounts at Wespath. Personnel at the Wespath will typically invest the funds based on the age and years of service of the contributor, just as they do for the defined contribution plan. But, it is entirely possible for an individual to invest it him- or herself, but only in funds available at Wespath. Laity are also allowed to participate in this plan.

As with the defined contribution plan, even modest contributions can grow quickly, even if the market causes a decline in any particular year.

Taken together, these three forms of employer-provided retirement can be very effective. For United Methodists who have access to one of each of the three types of plans, they can quickly build a significant balance in the defined contribution plan and the UMPIP 403(b) plan. Upon retirement, these accounts would all be available to assist a retiree trying to live on the check provided by the defined benefit plan. In addition, the retiree would have full access to Social Security. With all of these components working together, retirees have income that may be reduced from that to which they were accustomed, but not so low that it precludes continuing in generosity and ministry, not to mention feeling secure and satisfied in retirement. Someone who saves significantly in the individual savings plans might even find more income than he or she had before retiring.

For more information on Social Security, see my website www.nateberneking.com.

Individual Forms of Retirement Savings

I have in no way exhausted the possibilities for savings. Even part-time pastors and laity serving in remote rural churches, working in small businesses, or pursuing a sole-proprietorship have opportunities to save. In these sorts of settings, individuals aren't likely to have access to any sort of company-run pension or savings plans. There will be no 401(k) or 403(b), no defined benefit or defined contribution. Instead, the individual will be solely responsible for his or her own retirement, but they will at least receive some assistance from the government through tax relief, with a general administrative structure from a bank.

Individuals without the option of other plans should first consider some form of an *individual retirement account* or "IRA." IRAs take two basic forms: traditional or Roth. A traditional IRA allows an individual to contribute up to $5,500, excluding that entire amount from income for purposes of calculating tax.[2] In other words, the IRA allows people to shelter a small amount of income from tax, while also saving for retirement. Banks typically administer IRAs, allowing customers to make deposits as they do with checking and savings accounts, providing them with statements and, when available, online access to account administration. Even the smallest of local banks are likely to have options. In large banks, the amounts contributed to the IRA can even be invested in a portfolio of stocks, bonds, or mutual funds. This allows individuals to place their retirement savings in investments as if they were contributed to a 401(k) or 403(b). The tax treatment is just as advantageous (no tax is paid until one takes distributions). But, early withdrawal penalties can be just as stiff as they are for 401(k) or 403(b) accounts. In other words, unless one has a dire emergency, money contributed to a traditional IRA should be left in the account until at least age 59 1/2. At that point, individuals may begin making withdrawals, and once investors reach 70 1/2 years of age they *must* begin taking distributions. Any bank or investment company can explain the intricacies of these rules and assist in establishing one.

---

2. The IRS does limit IRA contributions based on a taxpayer's Adjusted Gross Income, a concept that will be defined in chapter 4. Here, it is sufficient to say that AGI is comprised of an individual's total income reduced by a few deductions universally offered to qualifying taxpayers, and that contributors to IRAs should consult professionals to be sure they receive the full benefit of any contributions.

Roth IRAs work in much the same way as traditional IRAs, but with different tax treatment. In these accounts, contributions by the individual are not exempt from income tax. Instead, the Roth IRA shelters the money from tax upon distribution. The advantage of such an account is that the individual pays no tax on distributions, and that includes the entire return earned by the investments over the life of the account. Recalling the family in chapter 2, suppose Jack deposits $3,000 in a Roth IRA when he's thirty. Assuming a 5 percent annual return over the life of the IRA, he will have $12,950 in the IRA when he is sixty. At that point, he may begin taking distributions. In a Roth, he would have paid taxes on the $3,000 he contributed, as it was part of his total income, but no distribution will be taxed when he is sixty, including the more than $9,000 he earned. If Jack contributed $3,000 to the Roth every year during the thirty-year period, the amount of return will be much higher, and entirely shielded from taxes.

While the caps on contributions are much higher for employer-administered plans, individuals have good options for retirement savings even if their employer is a small church with no plan. Subject to certain limits imposed by the IRS, pastors in The United Methodist Church may have the option of contributing to both IRAs and their pension plan. This may be unnecessary, especially given that tax advantages in IRAs begin phasing out when an employee is receiving similar treatment in an employer plan, but my experience suggests that employees are apt to utilize too few investment options, rather than too many. For that reason, any pastor who asks whether a Roth or traditional IRA is a good option receives the same answer: "If you contribute enough to your United Methodist pension, you may not need it, but more retirement savings, in any sort of account, is always good. But, always be sure to consult tax and financial planning professionals."

Before turning to the theological justifications, I want to comment on one additional savings mechanism that isn't exactly for retirement but is likely to have a significant effect on the financial health of anyone with children. This book doesn't particularly address college savings, but for any church leader with children, such an effort is critical. As with retirement options, any vehicle used to save money and obtain a rate of return will be helpful to defray the ever-increasing costs of secondary education. That said, the US government has created a mechanism that allows parents (or even grandparents) to save for their children's education and obtain tax savings, though in a different way than with IRAs.

Qualified *529 Plans* are federally authorized, state-created plans that allow individuals to contribute to college savings. Earnings and distributions are exempt from *federal* income tax. In some states, the investment returns in the plans have been less than optimal. But, in a few, states have used reputable mutual fund investments and provide helpful state income tax exemptions for contributions to the 529 plan. A few states allow state tax exemptions for contributions made to the 529 plans of other states. My own state of Missouri has maximized the use of its own 529, called Missouri MOST.

Contributions work much like an IRA. Individuals make contributions, often utilizing an online platform to make deposits directly from a bank account. Account holders must establish a beneficiary. That beneficiary may be a child or grandchild with future aspirations for college. Once contributed, amounts must be used for qualified tuition, room and board, or other education costs. In other words, the amounts are restricted. If the restrictions are followed, no tax is imposed upon withdrawals. If money is withdrawn for any other purpose, the withdrawal is taxed and penalized, though often an exception is made when a student receives a full-ride scholarship, eliminating tuition.

The restriction on use does raise questions with respect to the risk of these plans. If your child decides not to go to college, something becoming more common, the money would appear to be locked up. Fortunately, contributors have options. First, they may simply change the beneficiary, naming a child or grandchild who might use the funds for college. If your child doesn't go to college, their child might. Second, many simply choose to leave the money in place. There are no time or age restrictions. The child who chooses not to go to college at nineteen might make a different decision at thirty. Parents and grandparents making contributions must make peace with the idea that the money contributed is for future generations, and might be used differently than was intended. For these reasons, I still think a 529, at least in the right state, provides a great mechanism to save on behalf of a child, insulating other assets that might be needed in retirement.

II. A Theological Approach to Saving

Jesus called them and immediately they left the boat and their father and followed him.

—Matthew 4:21-22

Earn all you can. Save all you can. Give all you can.[3] That's not quite how Wesley phrased it, but he definitely preached a sermon

---

3. See John Wesley's sermon "The Use of Money," in *John Wesley's Sermons:*

centered on those ideas. As a student of the Bible, especially in seminary, I always looked askance at the notion of earning and saving. I'm not sure that's really what Jesus had in mind, especially given what he said to the rich young ruler and Zacchaeus. Giving away all one's possession or even half of them doesn't seem to square with the notion of retirement savings. Let's look at a story I find particularly troubling for anyone trying to save for retirement.

In Matthew 4:18-22, Jesus called his disciples. In this short passage, we have two significant episodes. First, he approached Peter and Andrew. They were working at established careers, fishing. I've done my share of fishing, at least with a rod and reel. At different times in my life, I'd even say that I've been passionate about fishing. My passion notwithstanding, I am well aware that the only certainty in fishing is that there is no certainty. On one trip, fishing alone, I found myself catching one good-sized trout after another. On the very next trip to the same river, hiring a guide I knew to have had great success, being told where to cast for the best chance, taught how to cast properly, I caught exactly one, too small to keep. I can't count the number of times I've fished, with fishermen more skilled than I, and never once felt even a bite. I recognize that fishing with nets in the ocean and fishing with rods and reels are two very different activities. Nets in heavily populated fisheries are more likely to pull in a catch, but even then, weather, temperature, and faulty equipment can easily leave the commercial fishermen empty-handed. That Peter and Andrew were fishermen is significant. They were employed in a difficult, high-risk career.

Maybe that made the decision to follow Jesus easier, but I think it's remarkable that he said he would make them fish for people. As

An Anthology, ed. Albert Outler and Richard Heitzenrater (Nashville: Abingdon, 1991), 335–46.

a pastor, I've fished for people, too. I know what it is to strike up a conversation with a stranger, heart fluttering, finding questions and statements to keep the conversation going, explaining that I'm a pastor (not slimy like the ones on TV) and finally, sometimes after several conversations, getting around to, "You know, if you would be interested, I'd like to invite you to church this Sunday, to be my guest, no pressure, but I think you'd enjoy it." They always respond the same way: "Yeah, sure, I'd like that. I really have been meaning to get the family to church. What time does it start? Great. I'm looking forward to it." And then, when we part, "Great, I'll see you Sunday." I think I'm pretty good at fishing for people, but my success rate is significantly lower than I have fishing for fish. At least fish get trapped on a hook. Fishing for people is hard. Ask my bishop, Bishop Bob Farr, who writes books on evangelistic strategies.[4] If there's anything riskier than fishing for fish, it's fishing for people. Yet, when Jesus asked, Simon and Andrew dropped their nets and immediately followed Jesus.

They left careers and livelihoods. Perhaps they left uncertain income, but the life for which they opted was even more uncertain in what it promised. Before the story was over, it landed Jesus on a cross and the rest of them running scared.

This passage gets even more interesting. After Simon and Andrew chose to follow, Jesus approached James and John. They were also pursuing their trade, fishing. The exchange appears, at first glance, to be exactly the same as Simon and Andrew. But, here, Matthew added one detail. James and John were not working alone. They were with their father. Apparently, for Zebedee, fishing was a family business. In an ancient Mediterranean fishing business, I can guarantee, there was only one retirement plan: to have children.

4. Bob Farr, *Get Their Name* (Nashville: Abingdon, 2014).

People worked until they could work no more. Life was brutish and short anyway, but to keep oneself nourished, a person had to have children to take over the work when they came of age. James and John were the only retirement Zebedee had. All four early disciples left their futures in fishing when they followed. But when James and John dropped their nets, they didn't just let go of their livelihood. They rendered their father's future just as uncertain.

What does this say about retirement? About saving and accumulating wealth? Jesus and his first followers were nomadic teachers and holy people. They went around sharing a message. Boiled down to its essence, the message was simple: the world is safer than you thought. Despite poverty, pain, disease, famine, uncertainty, even agony, God cares and will provide. To overcome one's own sin and even death itself, one only need place his or her confidence in the notion that God cared so much for the world, that God's own self came to dwell in it. The first church leaders lived in a similar manner. For Paul, the idea that God entered the world, faced death itself, and defeated it, drove him to become a traveling apostle, living on the kindness of strangers, taking his message to as many places as he could get. We can't say for sure, but I can't imagine that with that attitude and practice, Paul ever saved for retirement. In fact, when it came to wealth, even comfort, Paul had a message not all that different from Jesus's. He wrote of learning the skill of contentment, no matter what a person had. In Philippians 4:12, he wrote, "I know the experience of being in need and of having more than enough; I have learned the secret to being content in any and every circumstance, whether full or hungry or whether having plenty or being poor." I doubt he saved for retirement.

Should we? It's easy to simply declare that life is different now than it was for Paul and Jesus's first disciples. Unfortunately, too many people today are so preoccupied with wealth that they never actually drop their nets to follow Jesus. In our culture, wealth and possessions are even more seductive than they were for the deeply impoverished people Jesus reached with his first message. We live in a culture of materiality and possession, a culture that insists that the only safe means of living is ensuring we have enough to shield ourselves from the discomforts of not having enough. But, Paul insisted we should be content regardless of our possessions.

Church leaders, clergy included, fall victim to the thinking of our culture. They seek to earn as much as they can and hoard money and possessions for their retirement years, years they plan to spend living comfortably, doing as they please, finally unleashed from the ministries they served. On the other hand, I know pastors who refuse to think or talk about retirement, using Jesus's nomadic lifestyle and ministry to the poor to justify their own refusal to deal with anything financial. Don't get me wrong, most pastors fall somewhere between these caricatures. Those who save carefully have often worked extremely hard. And those who refuse to discuss it have often given with extreme generosity.

At the same time, something doesn't quite sit right when it comes to either approach. I want to take Jesus and Paul seriously. Can we justify saving for retirement at all?

Perhaps Wesley was on to something, even if he gave a little too much credence to earning and saving. The whole point of Wesley's sermon was his final admonition: "give all you can." He embodied this himself, working with extreme energy over his entire life, but dying with almost no money to his own name. This should be our model for ministry. A paycheck can really mess up our idea of what ministry is supposed to be. Few of us decided to become pastors to collect that paycheck. Laity seem to do better keeping this straight. They don't volunteer their time and make contributions to the church in exchange for pay. They do it because they find it changes their lives and the lives of others for the better.

Ministry finds its beginning in the message shared by Jesus and his first followers: the world is safer than you thought. God cares for the world so much that God's own self came to dwell in it, facing death, defeating it, allowing us all to live better, to really live. If that's our message, our work in sharing that message doesn't stop when we turn sixty-five. Ministry is lifelong.

I'll admit, our brand of Christianity is a little different than Paul's. The earliest Christians had an apocalyptic slant. They believed Jesus was returning soon and that God would set the world to right in their lifetime. It would be a sin to stop hoping for that, but at the same time, after two thousand years, it has become clear, part of God's call on our lives is to hope for Christ's return, the salvation of the world, and another part is to wait, watch, and be prepared for ministry throughout life.

In this setting, if ministry is lifelong, it might be wise to ensure we have the resources needed to conduct it until we die. In Paul's day, he did that by relying on the kindness of strangers. In the contemporary United States, one might live a powerful ministry through a homeless, nomadic life, but doing so would be highly countercultural and only the most talented are likely to effectively share the good news with such an approach. Most people will need to enculturate themselves, providing for themselves the way most of the population does.

In this sort of culture, it makes good sense to be intentional about ensuring the resources you need for ministry over the course of your whole life. To justify retirement savings, I'm really marrying the central idea of chapter 1 to that of chapter 2. In chapter 1, I made it clear, the central activity of ministry should be generosity, opening ourselves to what God might be doing, living as if we really believe the world is safer than we thought, that God is closer than we knew. In chapter 2, I suggested that we ought to take our primary financial resources and plan for the ways we are going to be generous. We want to ensure that each year, we have enough to nourish ourselves while also being as generous as we can be. Intentionality is the only way we can grow to realize we nourish ourselves with more than we need, we entertain ourselves too exorbitantly, and we can almost always find ways to be more generous. Here, in chapter 3, I want to suggest that we should be just as intentional in considering our ministry over the course of our whole lives. We must realize that at some point, we will no longer receive a regular paycheck. To stay in ministry, we will still need resources. To continue living generously, we will need something to give. It only makes sense to plan for our retirement so we can do this after paychecks stop.

Retirement planning shouldn't be about amassing wealth. Its central activity should be reflecting on what we might do following retirement, how we might continue to serve the Church. For some, that might mean taking a part-time or interim appointment. For others, it will mean finding a local church where they can give and support the ministries led by the current pastor. Laypeople ought to reflect on how they might shift their ministry following their departure from their careers. After all, prior to retirement, ministry shouldn't be confined only to church activities. Laypeople should explore ways to be in ministry even at work. Once they stop working, they must find a way to reorient their ministry. For some, that might mean volunteering in homeless shelters or other service organizations. For others, it might be spending time in local diners or coffee shops, talking, even counseling strangers and staff. Pastors might take on the same roles. Regardless, doing this sort of work after retirement requires resources, and those resources will be reduced if one doesn't plan for finances after the paycheck stops.

This is why we should save all we can. It allows us to continue the practice of generosity. We must stay aware that God is close, that we need not worry about wealth. We must stand ready and willing to drop our livelihoods for the sake of Christ. At the same time, doing that doesn't preclude good planning. Retirement savings should only ever be about the intentionality needed to plan good ministry.

Chapter 4

Personal Taxes: Income, Social Security, and Medicare Taxes for Individuals

April is the cruelest month, breeding
Lilacs out of the dead land, mixing
Memory and desire, stirring
Dull roots with spring rain."[1]

Before converting to Christianity, T. S. Eliot was a bit of a cynic. For the Christian, spring and rebirth enliven our senses. If that means suffering with reignited nerve endings, it also means we experience joy, rendering the season better than death. For the Christian, life is always better than death.

Still, Eliot had a point. The first light we see in the morning hurts our rested eyes. Muscles ache from the previous day's work. Bones crack. Household activity exacerbates the pain. I, for one,

1. T. S. Eliot, "The Waste Land," in *The Waste Land and Other Poems* (New York: Harvest, 1962), 29.

need time and space before accepting the stimulation inherent in daily life.

So go seasons. In winter, we sleep longer, nestled under blankets, warming ourselves by fires, when suddenly, the first weeds emerge, allergies flare, and mowing becomes essential. Much as we love spring, warm weather, and longer days, it takes a few weeks to get used to it. The added life requires more work that few enjoy. To make matters worse, the federal government, not to mention many states, requires us to make a full accounting of our previous year's income, assessing a tax on it, compelling us to pay. By May, I'm enjoying the flowers and moderate temperatures. But April? April—with the extra work, waking up to new activity, collecting of financial documents, and forking over my previous year's taxes—is just too vile. Perhaps Eliot *was* right. April *is* the cruelest month. I strongly advise we learn how to prepare for it.

I. Practices and Patterns of Tax Preparation

Pastors remain baffled by a unique tax situation, which is why this chapter will focus on how the US tax system affects clergy. However, I'll still describe the basic tax situation for all individual and married taxpayers, hopefully making this chapter of general assistance. I'll focus only on federal taxes. Finally, the purpose of this chapter, and the book in general, is not to make an expert of readers. When it comes to tax preparation, my best advice is to seek help from a professional. At the very least, use the knowledge presented here to prepare your own taxes using a quality software product. Going it alone just isn't a good idea.

Regardless of how we make preparations, everyone employed in the United States must prepare for two kinds of federally imposed taxes: income tax and Social Security/Medicare taxes. Other sorts of taxes, those applying to capital gains from investments or corporate ownership, may or may not apply to church leaders. Again, to avoid topics too complex for this book, I'm going to focus only on the two that almost everyone must prepare and pay.

Federal Income Tax

The US government imposes a tax on nearly every sort of income. There are exceptions, but in most cases, taxes really are as certain as death. Most people experience income tax through payroll withholding and annual return filing. Payroll withholding is accomplished by the completion of a *Form W-4* required of employees in the United States. The employer then deducts a percentage of the employee's paychecks and pays it to the Treasury Department. Pastors complete a W-4 but do not have tax withheld in paychecks unless they do so voluntarily. Individuals who do not have enough withheld must make quarterly payments using a form called a *1040-ES*. The Internal Revenue Service, the agency responsible for collecting US taxes, requires that taxpayers pay taxes consistently throughout the year, whether via payroll deductions or quarterly estimated payments. Every individual must then file a return by April 15. On the return, we account for income, calculating tax, reducing it by amounts already withheld or paid. If the taxpayer still owes, he or she must make a payment. If the taxpayer paid too much during the year, the Treasury will refund the difference.

This is how federal income taxes are paid and collected. It's easy enough. Having to pay upon filing the April return is never pleasant, but for many anticipating a refund, completing and filing the return is the most painful part of the process. They must pay a preparer or obtain costly software. Worse, they set out to do it themselves and spend hours spinning wheels, adding numbers that make no sense, reading dense instructions, losing hours from life that no one ever gets back. If we're all required to pay, if we all face the prospect of completing and filing a return, perhaps it's best to reduce the agony, to understand more than we might wish. Here, as much as anywhere in this book, we might need to make a commitment to be more vile.

We start with income. What is income? Almost everything we receive during the year. Income primarily includes salaries, wages, and/or tips. But, if you gained interest from a bank account you owned, that counts. If you owned a house and rented it to another person, the rent counts. If you, God forbid, went to a casino and won a fortune playing blackjack . . . that counts, too. If you gained it, you can almost be sure that Uncle Sam includes it in the definition of income.

The definition of income in the Internal Revenue Code (26 U.S.C. §61 for those who want to look it up) includes almost everything we gain. Fortunately for pastors, there are a couple things that aren't included, and those things provide us with a favorable tax situation. First, we have no obligation to pay taxes of any sort on gifts that fall below $14,000. If your parents, your grandparents, your rich uncle, or a very kind member of your church gives you $500 (or even $5,000) at Christmas, you don't have to include that in the income on which you pay tax.

One exception to the rule on gifts does offer a risk to pastors and churches. As we'll see in chapter 8, churches must guard against any of their assets *inuring* to the benefit of private individuals. This is a legal way of saying that churches have limits on money given directly to individuals. This holds especially true for employees.

Churches may want to give a gift to the pastor, but this sort of giving is almost always taxable. If the congregation takes up a collection and gives it to the pastor, the pastor has received *income* from his or her employer. It must be taxed. That said, if a single church member privately offers a gift to the pastor, such amounts are not considered income and may be treated as gifts. The same analysis applies to pastors receiving honoraria for weddings and funerals. Typically, the IRS will treat these honoraria as fees paid to the pastor or as income from the local church, and they are taxed.

Second, amounts or accommodations provided to *clergy* in the form of *housing* are not included as income. In other words, a parsonage or housing allowance is certainly a form of compensation. But, because the church offers it as housing for a member of the clergy, pastors do not have to recognize any value of housing as income.[2] The IRS imposes limits on this, but those limits are quite high. A pastor may exclude from income any value of housing so long as the amount does not exceed the lowest of (a) the fair rental value of the home in which the pastor lives, fully furnished with all utilities paid; (b) the amount officially declared and adopted by the church/organization employing the pastor; and (c) the amount that can be substantiated with receipts or documentation by the pastor.

That might seem confusing, but it's easy. Clergy may receive a house and/or amounts used for the purpose of acquiring housing.

---

2.   At the time of writing, the statute allowing clergy to exempt housing related income from income tax (26 U.S.C. sec. 107) has been challenged in Federal Court. The Freedom From Religion Foundation contends that the exemption, offered only to clergy, violates the US Constitution's First Amendment Establishment Clause and Fourteenth Amendment Equal Protection Clause. See *Gaylor et al. v. Lew et al.,* Case No. 16-CV-215 (W.D. Wis. 2016). The same court previously agreed with the Freedom From Religion Foundation's argument, but was reversed on appeal to the 7th Circuit Court of Appeals on technical grounds. But, the most recent case has not yet been decided. Clergy should consult a tax and legal professional to discern how the outcome of this case might affect their taxes.

The church must approve exactly what's provided as housing. And for anything other than an actual house, the pastor must retain a record to substantiate. If a pastor pays the electric bill with amounts provided by the church as housing, he or she must keep the receipt or risk losing that much of the exemption in an audit. Just about anything spent to provide a home can be counted. Housing can even include furnishings of the home and utilities. If a pastor has the church designate the amount, he or she may exclude anything spent on utilities, furniture, small appliances, big appliances, home repairs, home renovations, lawn care, and basic maintenance. I always tell pastors that the definition isn't that exact, and to employ a standard of reasonableness. The IRS allows churches to provide pastors with a home. The home includes more than just the structure. That said, the pastor must keep receipts, avoid abusing the exemption, and always stay under the fair rental value of the home, fully furnished with utilities paid. How do you know the fair rental value? Again, use a reasonableness standard. If you are somehow excluding $50,000 from income for your home, and rents in your neighborhood are no more than $12,000 annually, you may be pushing the limits. If you're excluding $22,000 from income, using $12,000 as rent to a landlord or as a home mortgage payment, and then using $6,000 to purchase furniture, pay for home repairs, lawn care, and other maintenance, and the final $4,000 for utilities, then you are complying with the requirements. This exemption can be an exceptional tax savings for pastors.

Other important items that aren't counted as income include amounts paid by the employer for group health insurance plans, as well as certain contributions to pension plans. These can also assist people in reducing tax liability and assisting with retirement planning.

The total of all income is referred to as *gross income*. For most people, their salaries or wages will establish their gross income, salaries reported to them by their employer on a form called a W-2. The amount to include on the tax form is found in Box 1 of the W-2. The IRS also requires taxpayers to report all other income, and taxpayers are solely responsible to know if something must be reported or not. This means, no one can ever claim they didn't know an amount was supposed to be reported. When in doubt, count it.

Once gross income is established, the IRS allows a few items to be subtracted as *deductions*. Deductions fall into two categories. Some deductions are available to anyone who qualifies. Most tax preparers refer to these as *above the line* deductions. What line? Line 37 of the 1040. Once these deductions are subtracted from gross income, taxpayers are to report the amount in line 37, an amount known as *adjusted gross income* or AGI. AGI is often used as a standard to determine when taxpayers qualify for certain government programs and incentives. The above the line deductions include interest paid on student loans and amounts contributed to an IRA (remember our discussion from chapter 3). Methodist pastors who aren't reimbursed for moving expenses can deduct them here. Finally, contributions to a qualified *health savings account*, an account that's part of a growing number of health insurance plans, are also deductible above the line.

Once AGI is calculated, the taxpayer is given a choice for further deductions: standard or itemized. Everyone is entitled to reduce AGI by a *standard deduction*. In 2017, the standard deduction for individuals is $6,350. For those married and filing joint returns, the standard deduction is $12,700. A few taxpayers who qualify for a special filing status will have a standard deduction of $9,350.

However, church leaders and pastors, at least those who tithe, are typically entitled to deduct a greater amount than the standard deduction. The IRS allows taxpayers to deduct the greater of the standard deduction or qualified *itemized deductions*, with contributions to recognized charitable organizations providing one of the most significant itemized deductions.

Recall in chapter 2 that Sally made about $45,000 in cash and another $18,000 in housing allowance. Jack made $53,000 in hourly wages, received about $500 in investment returns, and received a generous gift of $5,000 from his parents each year. The total of their income is $121,500. If they tithe, they would make a yearly contribution to their church of more than $12,000, almost equal to the standard deduction they would receive if they gave nothing. Any extra contributions they make will qualify them for greater itemized deductions than the available standard deduction.

Taxpayers also commonly deduct interest paid on a loan used to acquire or refinance their home. Many pastors serve settings in which purchasing a home makes little sense. But, for some, and certainly for lay leaders, purchasing a home may allow for even greater itemized deductions. The interest on the loan used to finance the purchase is entirely tax deductible. That doesn't eliminate the cost of such interest entirely, but it does provide a significant reduction in what that interest will actually cost. Suppose Jack and Sally purchased a modest $170,000 home in their community, financing it with $150,000 borrowed from the local bank. When they took that home loan, the bank filed a special document called a *mortgage* or *deed of trust* with the local Recorder of Deeds office. This means that if Jack and Sally ever fail to make payments on the loan, the bank will be able to seize ownership from them through a process called *foreclosure*. This arrangement is key to a taxpayer's ability to deduct interest.

Currently, interest rates in the United States are very low. If Jack and Sally have good credit ratings, they might qualify for a loan today with an interest rate as low as 3.67 percent. If that's the case, then in the first year of their loan, they would make principal and interest payments of about $780 a month. This does not include additional amounts the bank would charge for property taxes and a special kind of insurance used by banks for first-time borrowers. In that first year, very little of the $780 would actually be comprised of principal (payments toward the debt of $150,000 itself). Most of the payment would be comprised of interest or the amounts paid for the privilege of using the bank's money to purchase the home.

In fact, in the first year, using a special calculator to figure how much interest they would pay, Jack and Sally would be entitled to deduct nearly $6,200 more from their AGI as an itemized deduction for interest paid on their home loan. With charitable donations, that brings their itemized deductions to more than $18,000, well over the standard deduction.

There are numerous rules related to itemizing deductions. Rather than listing every itemized deduction and providing the rules for their use, my intent is simply to provide the reader with an understanding of how they work to reduce AGI.

A more complete list of itemized deductions can be found at www.nateberneking.com.

Once itemized or standard deductions reduce AGI, taxpayers arrive at an amount referred to as *taxable income*. This is the amount on which we actually pay tax. From this amount, the taxpayer (or more likely the software) refers to *tax tables* to obtain the tax owed.

Federal income tax is known as a progressive tax, meaning that taxpayers earning more will pay a greater percentage of their income than those earning less. However, the highest rate is currently capped and rates only increase for income in excess of the previous level. The federal income tax begins at a flat 10 percent, applying to people with taxable income below $9,325 ($18,650 if married). Any income received between $9,325 and $37,950 ($75,900 if married) is then taxed at 15 percent. From there, the tax rates continue to step up to a maximum of 39.6 percent. Most full-time pastors will only have taxable income falling in brackets of 10, 15, and 25 percent.

Suppose Jack and Sally are able to reduce their taxable income through above the line and itemized deductions to $72,000. They would pay federal income tax equaling 10 percent of all amounts up to $18,650 plus 15 percent of amounts between $18,651 and $75,900.

> 10 percent of the first $18,650   = $1,865
> 15 percent of ($72,000 - 18,650) = $8,003

This means Jack and Sally owe the total of each bracket amount or $9,868 ($1,865 + $8,003). That's a great deal of money owed to the US Treasury. Fortunately, Jack and Sally wouldn't be finished calculating what they actually owe. The amount of tax is then reduced by various credits, the most critical of which includes the amounts they've already paid through payroll deductions or quarterly estimated amounts. For pastors, payroll deductions do not come automatically. They must be requested when completing a Form W-4. Pastors who have nothing withheld must pay amounts to the IRS quarterly, estimating their tax that will be owed (the previous year is usually a good guide), and splitting the estimate into four equal payments on January 15, April 15 (same day as the return is required), June 15, and September 15. Pastors especially should understand that the IRS requires payment throughout the year, whether through payroll or estimated quarterly payments. If a taxpayer owes the IRS more than $1,000 when he or she files the required tax return in April, the IRS will impose a small, but painful, penalty.

In addition to amounts already paid, parents are entitled to a *child tax credit* of $1,000 for each of their children. The credit begins to be phased out for families with AGI exceeding certain amounts. Even for taxpayers with a portion of the credit eliminated, the amount can result in significant savings.

For working taxpayers who earn very little, the earned income credit "EIC" represents a significant subsidy provided by the US government. In order to receive it, taxpayers must complete the appropriate forms and file for it with their tax returns. The US government saves itself millions every year because qualified taxpayers simply fail to take advantage and these lower income individuals fail to obtain free money.

As with deductions, the tax code allows for many credits that don't apply to most people. A conversation with a tax professional or the use of software that ensures availability of the correct credits is absolutely critical to avoiding unnecessary taxes. This is just good stewardship. I never advocate illegally avoiding taxes, but legally and ethically reducing what we pay only frees up more of our resources for use in our ministry.

Social Security Tax

Federal income tax isn't the only tax owed to the US government. Most working Americans pay an additional tax without even

73

realizing it, taking the amounts paid for granted until they retire. The United States has extensive and interlocking systems operating as public pensions and health insurance for retirees, systems known popularly as Social Security and Medicare. At different times in the last few years, these systems have been alternately praised and vilified. My hope is to avoid the controversy. The truth of such matters is to be found somewhere other than in the mouths of politicians, hopeful for votes. The truth is, Social Security and Medicare are costly, but provide income and health care for many people who wouldn't otherwise have enough to even meet basic needs. How or whether we continue to utilize such systems is beyond the scope of my project. I simply want to discuss how they affect pastors and leaders in our local churches.

To fund Social Security and Medicare, Congress adopted the *Federal Insurance Contributions Act* ("FICA") in the 1950s and an accompanying *Medicare Tax* in the 1960s. Social Security works much the way employer-defined benefit plans work, as discussed in chapter 3. Through contributions and tax, people pay part of their paycheck into large funds invested for the purpose of meeting future obligations. Retirees who have paid in are entitled to receive a set benefit through Social Security and basic health insurance through Medicare. Neither benefit is designed to provide for an exorbitant lifestyle. Even people who worked for decades receive modest checks from Social Security. Medicare doesn't nearly cover every medical need for the normal retiree. This means that most Americans must also save for their own retirement and be ready to purchase additional health insurance to pay for what Medicare doesn't cover. Still, that Americans have such benefits through government funding ought to be remarkable. But, they aren't free.

FICA requires every employer to withhold 6.2 percent of each employee's paycheck. The Medicare Tax requires an additional 1.45 percent. For ordinary employees, employers must then match both amounts, paying the withheld amount and the match to the IRS through what are called "payroll taxes." If you do the math, employees have 7.65 percent withheld and employers match that with an additional 7.65 percent, bringing the total to 15.3 percent of each paycheck.

Most working people barely notice the deduction, seeing it only when they actually read the stubs of paychecks.

When I teach a clergy tax class, I like to tell participants that this is how the process *normally* works. Unfortunately, and I think I'm safe in saying this as one in solidarity, clergy are seldom "normal." In the case of Social Security, clergy aren't alone. In the 1950s, when Congress adopted FICA, they realized that the contributions process would only work for individuals employed by an organization or other individual. Some people work on their own. Some people are *self-employed*. Congress also realized that most churches, at least at the time, had only one employee, the pastor. Congress also realized just how difficult a time churches had in figuring out matters of finance and administration. Finally, Congress understood that some religious traditions objected to social welfare from secular government. Many Amish and Mennonite groups insisted that the Christian community had an obligation for its own retirees, wanting to stay separate from the US government. For all these reasons, Congress made two significant decisions with respect to clergy.

First, clergy in traditions with a clear objection to social welfare are allowed to opt out of Social Security entirely. To do this, clergy must complete a Form 4361, on which he or she certifies opposition to public insurance. By doing this, the pastor opts out of Social Security for good. While it's true that the IRS occasionally holds a period of amnesty in which pastors who opted out and later wish back in are allowed, the general rule is that once out, the pastor must stay out. The pastor must also make this decision within two years of receiving income as a member of the clergy. The IRS and Congress plainly adopted a policy that released people from traditions with religious objections to secular government to opt out. The idea was never to allow pastors to opt out for financial reasons or because they have the idea that Social Security costs too much or that it will fail at some point in the future. Clergy are only allowed out if they have religious objections to public insurance.

In fact, for United Methodists, opting out should be extremely rare. Any pastor who pays lip service to the Social Principles of The United Methodist Church can't make the necessary certification. The United Methodist Church, especially in the Social Principles, seems to support the government's effort to provide for public insurance.[3] In fact, The United Methodist Church bases its entire pension program on the fact that clergy are to receive three streams of income in retirement: (a) income from the defined benefit plan; (b) income from the retiree's defined contribution and personal investment plan; and (c) *Social Security.*

More significantly, Congress also decided that churches would not have to participate in the contributions process of FICA unless they had lay staff. Many of our churches have such staff today, even smaller ones, meaning that they regularly pay payroll taxes and deduct FICA and Medicare Tax from employee paychecks. In the 1950s, however, that wasn't the case. Most churches, even mid-

---

3. *The 2012 United Methodist Book of Discipline* (Nashville: United Methodist Publishing, 2012), Para. 162(F).

sized and larger churches, only employed a pastor. Instead of burdening churches with the practice of payroll withholding and taxes, Congress declared self-employed status for clergy. Subsequently, the IRS has clarified that pastors are only self-employed for purposes of Social Security and Medicare, meaning that they are employees of the local church for purposes of income tax. This means that they do not, as most self-employed, receive a Form 1099 from the church, an income form similar to a W-2, but meant for *independent contractors* who engage the organization. The pastor is *not* like the custodial contractor or organ tuner. He or she is not a contractor.

Pastors are employees for purposes of receiving a W-2. But, at the same time, pastors are self-employed for purposes of Social Security and Medicare Tax. This means that they won't have FICA or Medicare Tax withholdings from their paycheck.

But, Congress did not want to exclude the self-employed from public insurance programs that it saw as critical to the future of the United States. Because of that, Congress also passed the *Self-Employed Contributions Act* or "SECA." Sometimes people refer to SECA as the *self-employment tax*. How much must self-employed individuals pay into Social Security and Medicare? That ought to be obvious: 15.3 percent of their income, the combined amount paid by individual employees and their employers under FICA and the Medicare Tax. In other words, for self-employed individuals, the burden falls only on the individual. There is no sharing the tax with the employer because there isn't an employer other than one's own self.

This creates an odd scenario for pastors. They pay income tax, going through the process of receiving a W-2 and filing a 1040 like other employees. But, in addition to their 15–25 percent tax bracket, pastors must also pay 15.3 percent in self-employment taxes, often bringing their total effective tax rate to 25–35 percent of income. Worse, pastors don't have the 15.3 percent of SECA withheld from paychecks. They don't have it quietly disappear as others do with FICA. Instead, the 15.3 percent is due and payable either through voluntary payroll deductions, by way of quarterly estimated payments to the IRS, or on April 15. Many young pastors who fail to adequately make these voluntary payments have found themselves with an enormous tax bill in their first year of ministry.

Fortunately, the problem can be easily rectified. In fact, despite the heavy burden of SECA, pastors, if they plan, will still end up with a better tax situation than most Americans. In the previous section of this chapter, I explained that pastors are provided an exceptional benefit in the way of their housing. Pastors, at least in The United Methodist Church, must receive a rent-free parsonage or adequate housing allowance from the churches they serve. Better, the Internal Revenue Code explicitly excludes the rental value and/or allowance amounts from income tax. In other words, pastors actually receive much more income than what their W-2 shows. They avoid paying income taxes on their housing. Most people must pay for housing out of their regular salary. In the Missouri Annual Conference, the minimum salary allowed for a full-time, ordained pastor is just over $37,000 a year. The church must also pay an additional $10,000 in housing or provide rent-free use of a home meeting certain minimum standards. Likewise, the pastor receives pension contributions, death and disability insurance, and some form of health care, all of which, like housing, are excluded from income tax.

In reality, pastors are paid much more than they realize, especially when compared to people in other professions, at least those with analogous commitments to the common good of society. When I've compared similar cash salaries and done the tax math, I've found that pastors actually come out ahead of secular employees. They have a much more favorable situation despite bearing the entire burden for Social Security and Medicare.

I should add, maybe even in bold letters, the housing allowance or parsonage that is exempt from income tax, is *not* exempt from SECA. We must include it in the 15.3 percent calculation. If the pastor has a parsonage, he or she must determine the fair rental value and pay 15.3 percent of that fair rental value. Even with this, most pastors gain a benefit from the exemption of housing from income tax.

To reap these benefits, however, pastors must engage in planning and preparation. They must have more deducted from their paycheck or at least make estimated or voluntary payments using the math I laid out above. Come April 15, they'll be glad they did.

II. A Theological Approach to Paying Taxes

For the sake of the Lord submit to every human institution. . . . Submit to them because it's God's will that by doing good you will silence the ignorant talk of foolish people. . . . Honor everyone.

—1 Peter 2:13, 15, 17

The truth is, I get confused when it comes to Christian participation in secular systems. A serious student of the Bible recognizes that the authors, especially of the New Testament, never quite agreed on how Christians ought to approach secular government. In John's Revelation, the author takes as extreme a view as possible. Government, at least that of Rome, aligned itself with spiritual forces of wickedness. Therefore, Christians had to batten down the hatches, maintain low profiles, and refuse to participate. In other books of the Bible, authors indicated that the best approach to government was to blend in.

The letter of 1 Peter highlights the tension, stating clearly that Christians were to think of themselves as "immigrants" or "strangers" of the world in which they lived. As immigrants, they would want to hold strong to an identity given by their homeland—in this case, the kingdom ruled by Christ—but in order to make life easier, perhaps in order to validate and share their home identities, Christians ought also be wary of making waves in the secular community.

In Rome, this meant participating in the primary means of expressing patriotism, an act that other groups and generations of Christians had simply refused on the bases of prescriptions against idolatry, honoring the emperor. Roman authorities had used just such refusals as a common basis for arresting Christians in the past.

At the same time, there was more going on in 1 Peter than making life easier by participating in basic patriotic practices. Christians spent most of the first century trying to make sense of what had happened in Christ. They had to also spend time thinking and reflecting, making sense of the world in which they lived, a world dominated by an imperial government, one hostile to anything that questioned the authority and identity it imposed. Christianity wasn't born in comfortable circumstances. The story of the Gospels highlights this: baby born in a stable rather than a home, life roaming the countryside rather than based in a fixed location, ultimate victory through a shameful death on a cross rather than heroic victory. For the author of 1 Peter, it wasn't a significant jump to conclude that the way to salvation was to accept the circumstances in which one found one's self. In the case of the Christians to whom he wrote, that meant accepting the institutions that existed around them, understanding that God would work through those institutions, even those that caused suffering, in order to redeem the lives they lived.

How were they to do that? They were to live as immigrants. On the one hand, they were to avoid "worldly desires" that would erode their true identities in Christ. On the other, they were to "live honorably among unbelievers." The way of salvation was never to be through forced conversions or thrown insults. Christians were to exhibit honorable lives, lives shaped by Christ, by love, in the midst of the unbelieving world in which they lived. They were to be lights, demonstrating the way God would have all to live, while accepting that some would live differently. They were to tolerate and accept human institutions, assuming that God would work through those institutions, including changing them when the time was right.

I'm the last to suggest that Christians shouldn't work for justice. But, we must be wary of arrogance. Without God, we are powerless. Christians ought always to work and act in love, even for those with whom they disagree, even those they believe are acting badly. How that might shape our activities around justice has to be left for another day, but it suggests something about living in the United States. It suggests something about paying taxes, whether we should and how we should think about them when we do.

I'll confess, I'm not much of a patriot. I don't like the American flag in the sanctuary of a church. It doesn't belong. The pledge of allegiance isn't all that different from the homage that Romans were to pay to the emperor, substituting a piece of cloth vested with symbolic significance, for the likeness of a human being given ultimate authority. Sometimes, when I think about activities in which the United States has been involved, I cringe singing the National Anthem. And, like many my age, I question the practice of voting when I look around and see politicians in both established political parties behaving badly and taking positions that are anything but consistent with my Christian identity.

At the same time, I recognize significant benefits I've received as an American. Even when I've struggled the most financially, I've lived a middle-class existence, and when compared to 98 percent of the world's population, it can only be classified as an extremely wealthy existence.

Different groups of Christians question activities of the US or state governments in which they live, but it's hard to argue: nearly every facet of government has in some way provided enormous benefits. When I think about that, when I think about what I've received, when I think about the possibility that God might be working through every human institution, even the ones that clearly work against God's will, I think the exhortation in 1 Peter about living as an immigrant is a good one. And if that's the case, then taxes become part of the cost we pay in order to stay in the business of doing ministry, of living honorably among the unbelievers. If we are to be lights, demonstrating God's love in the midst of a hard, secular, sometimes evil world, then paying taxes will be necessary. We will be expected to pay a small homage to the country in which we live, to provide for benefits that others might enjoy. Refusing to do so, or objecting too loudly about them, will only ever earn us lost credibility.

Again, I'm not suggesting we should pay taxes blindly, never questioning US policy. We are still to be Christians, maintaining that identity. We have to keep ourselves free from legal and financial entanglements in order that the light of that true identity is most magnified for those we serve, for the communities in which we live. A mess with the IRS, especially one created by our own carelessness or intentional misdeeds, will only serve to damage our integrity before the churches and greater communities we serve.

As with budgeting and saving for retirement, paying taxes and understanding them as best we can are simply more ways we can support our posture of generosity. What if, instead of grumbling, procrastinating, or missing the deadlines, all church leaders entered tax season by reflecting on how they might save and what good they might do? What if we reflected on how paying taxes was necessary to stay in the good graces of our neighbors? Even better, what if understanding the process could assist with the greater community, perhaps allowing pastors and church leaders to offer support to individuals who struggle to understand?

Paying taxes is part of life. No matter what politicians might say, it won't go away. Don't get me wrong. I'm always suspicious of the person who pays his taxes without question, as an act of patriotism, a devotion to a god that is anything but the Creator. I'm devoted exclusively to the God in Christ, even if I fail in that devotion from time to time. Christians in America must be always wary of the cult of patriotism that exists, that occasionally even adopts Christian language to mask devotion to the idols it supports. On the other hand, I'm equally suspicious of the conscientious objector intentionally violating the law, withholding tax, convincing him- or herself that failing to pay taxes is somehow a contribution to a great cause—the avoidance of war, the feeding of the hungry,

83

justice for the oppressed. In those cases, people pay homage to a different but no more Christian god. Even worse is the disorganized, lazy sort that refuses to engage in something they just don't like, a nod only to the self, a sense that one's own proclivities might trump involvement in institutions that give meaning for much of society.

Paying taxes is and always has been an homage to a world and life littered with things we cannot change, a secular regime, a government with which we may not agree, but a world that ought always be understood as the world God created, and therefore, something we consider, understand, and engage carefully and intentionally.

Transition

I've in no way covered every facet of personal finance. In writing these chapters, I have realized just how significant and complicated an individual's personal finances might be. As with all facets of a Christian's life, holiness will always feel like a moving target. Just when one nails down the details needed to undertake greater generosity, something changes, another opportunity to give comes to light, and one more detail with respect to personal spending slides into mind.

I've not addressed the enormous topics of health care or socially responsible investing. I've not even addressed the details of how or where one might spend money. Instead, I've offered a mere glimpse into what holier living might look like and suggested a way to think about how our finances play a role. The key to holy living will always be an open and generous posture. I've tried to suggest that all personal financial considerations ought to be run through the question, "Is this allowing me to be more generous, more open to what God might be doing around me?" Asking that question leads us to be more intentional. This book isn't going to make you live better, but imagine getting your arms around an approach to generosity in your church and community, a personal budget, a plan for retirement savings, including a plan for how you'll continue in ministry, and deeper consideration of personal income taxes. Just those four aspects of financial life would go far in offering you stronger and more opportunities to be in ministry.

Those four aspects would be a step toward becoming a holier person. And, from there, we are able to step into the same sort of analysis needed to lead congregations. Financial leadership is critical for our congregations to find their own ways into holiness.

PART II

Holy Congregations

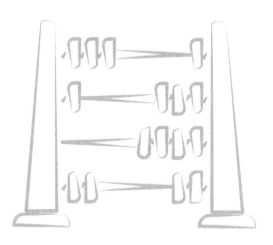

Chapter 5

Congregational Generosity: Practicing and Eliciting Trust

In his now decade-old book, Peter Scazzero wrote of "emotionally healthy churches," arguing that unhealthy leaders make for unhealthy congregations.[1] Healthy leaders lead healthy congregations. Scazzero's work transcends my own, but his arguments have as much validity in the specifics of personal and congregational finance and administration as they do in the more socio-emotional situations he addressed. The mature church leader and pastor recognize the need for good financial and administrative practices, learning what they need to be good leaders even when the topics are unattractive. The open posture and generosity with which I started marks the spiritual maturity Scazzero discusses more generally.

When congregations come together in healthy ways, miracles take place. People's lives are changed for the better. Healing and wholeness become hallmarks. On the other hand, because congregations are greater than the sum of their parts, when integration

---

1. Peter Scazzero, *The Emotionally Healthy Church: A Strategy for Discipleship That Actually Changes Lives* (Grand Rapids: Zondervan, 2010).

takes place in unhealthy ways, marked by the spiritually immature, problems take on a significance far surpassing that which they may have in an individual's life.

I spend a great deal of time in congregations and I consistently experience two primary problems. First, the vast majority of congregations relate that they are short on money needed to pay bills. They usually estimate a certain period of time for which they can pay their obligations. In many places, they report just a day or two's worth of *operating income*. Worse, many have experienced some conflict over money. Sometimes, they have reserves and leaders argue about how they ought to be used. Sometimes, leaders question the decisions made by others. In the worst cases, some wrongdoing has been identified.

I always ask the same thing: "How's the level of trust?" The answers vary, some honestly indicating that no one really trusts anyone else, the pastor least of all. Others assert that they really have no issue. In those cases, the pastor often pulls me aside to say something like, "I know what they said, but I've never felt trusted."

Unless leaders, lay and clergy, trust one another, the congregation will always suffer with administrative problems. If finance and administration are poorly or, worse, unethically conducted, a breach of trust will take years to heal, hindering the congregation's growth in ways from which it may not recover. If readers are part of a congregation that has already experienced that sort of breach, they will need to spend a great deal of time and intentional effort restoring trust before they can ever restore health.

Just as financial health in an individual's life must begin with a posture of openness and generosity, so goes congregational health. Generosity, trust, openness, and spiritual maturity really matter when it comes to whether or not a congregation thrives. If the individual leaders find their own financial and emotional health, such health will be magnified in the life of the congregation. Congregations, as individuals, must begin with generosity and openness.

I. Practices and Patterns of Congregational Generosity

A congregation's generosity is marked by practices. Bishop Robert Schnase gave language to this in *The Five Practices of Fruitful Congregations*, a work in which he urged "extravagance" in generosity.[2] Maybe it's obvious, but generosity will always be measured in terms of actual giving. One is only generous if one actually gives something. Congregational life follows suit. Whether a congregation is generous depends on whether it, as a whole, acts generously, and that depends a great deal on how it administers its finances.

I don't mean to entirely systematize generosity. Congregations may find countless ways to open themselves for the benefit of others. Rather, I have a few bare-minimum suggestions. The following characterize churches that I and others have found to be generous. These practices are found in churches large and small.

Prayer

Every publication on generosity and stewardship seems to start here. I only wish I could improve upon the suggestion. Generous congregations always include intentional prayer for their own generosity and the needs of others as part of any program of stewardship or fundraising.

---

2. Robert Schnase, *Five Practices of Fruitful Congregations* (Nashville: Abingdon, 2007), 123.

Many resources I've read have a shallow, even bankrupt theology of prayer when it comes to money. They suggest that praying for money will bring money. Some even identify the ridiculousness of that approach, while then implying the same understanding. I'm never quite satisfied when I hear a speaker or read an author who declares that prayer is necessary for successful fundraising. I don't always like capital campaign consultants who have pastors and lay leaders call every member of the church, offering to pray for them, while reminding them of the capital need and coming campaign. That seems manipulative.

I've also never seen a church develop a sense of generosity and openness *without* an intentional prayer life. I always present it like this: Assume that prayer has no supernatural effect. Assume that God just doesn't work like that, that there is no direct phone line. Then, imagine two congregations: one refuses to accept the skepticism, constantly praying to be generous, asking God to bless the local community and world through their work. They pray that God will make them more generous, that God will open them to do more, to give more, to work and serve more. Then, imagine a second congregation made of people who are only ever skeptical, who never pray for generosity, who simply attend worship and Sunday school, but never actually utter words of petition for more generosity or for more good work. Even if the skeptical church is right in its doubt, which congregation is more apt to be generous?

You don't have to have an understanding of prayer as a phone line to God. You might even doubt direct connection between petitions uttered and answers God gives. You might, as I often do, think of God as something transcendent, beyond our comprehension. You might even imagine God only in terms of mystery. In that case, our prayers are utterances of our desires that have their root in the mystery, but that require a partnership between the mystery and our own created, concrete selves to bring to fruition. Even if you have this less-magical concept of prayer, it is still absolutely critical to growing in generosity.

Prayer practices like meditation or labyrinth-walking are ways to tap into the mystery, ways of growing closer to the transcendent, whatever God might be. In making that connection, we find that we open ourselves. If connecting to God requires a posture of openness, nothing is more consistent than learning to be more generous, more open with our things and money. Prayer ought to always go hand-in-hand with giving. One practice (prayer) opens our souls to listen for the mystery. The other (giving) opens us in pragmatic ways, reminding us that the world is safer than we thought, that the mystery has the capacity to protect and hold and even provide us with all we might need.

When we pray, it has a way of opening us to more generosity. When we're generous, it opens us to the connection with God we ought always to seek in prayer. It will always be bad theology to assert that giving leads to blessing, to receiving more, to physical healing and health. At the same time, it would be careless to reject the connection between our sense of wholeness or health and how open our posture is with respect to God and others. For that reason, I start in the same place. Giving begins with intentional prayer. That's true for individuals. It's just as true, if not more so, for congregations. Whatever your program to increase giving and generosity, it must always start with a sense of connection to God, a connection that gains its most intimate expression in intentional prayer. Pray to be generous, and we might actually become so. Pray to be generous, and our congregation may become so.

Talking about Money

As with prayer, I wish I had something original to say about talking about money in church. Nobody likes to do it. It's vile. But, without it, a congregation's financial health can become so poor, that its very life will be threatened. In order to be generous, a congregation must learn to talk about money and their ability and desire to give it away.

Jesus seemed to have this idea that possessions, our things, have a way of becoming expressions of our identity.[3] When I was in my twenties, my grandmother gave me a quilt made by her mother (my great-grandmother) and aunt (my great-great-aunt). I was exceedingly close to my grandmother. That *she* gave me the quilt made it all the more powerful. I could have put the quilt away, keeping it in pristine condition, wrapped in plastic, or maybe even framed for display. I didn't. I did what a person is always supposed to do with a quilt. I use it. It keeps me warm and makes me feel secure, safe, loved. Suppose a burglar broke into my home and stole the quilt. How do you suppose I'd feel? Devastated.

In that quilt, I invested the identities of my grandmother, my great-grandmother, my great-great-aunt, my mother's entire family, even my identity. As with the quilt, all possessions have great capacity to serve as sacraments, signs in which the thing to which they point might be fully expressed, even present.

Photographs, cups, quilts, vases, jewelry all become expressions of people we love, as well as our own identity. There's just one problem. The New Testament, not to mention the Old, makes it very clear that we are to draw our identity from a single source. As long as the things we cherish point beyond ourselves and on to the God

---

3. Luke Timothy Johnson, *Sharing Possessions: What Faith Demands*, 2nd ed. (Grand Rapids: Eerdmans, 2011), 30–39.

who created us, everything is fine. Our problems start when we stop at our identities. At that point, our possessions become the means by which we try and protect, secure, and validate ourselves. Those are the role of God alone. Stepping into them makes us something none of us want to admit we are—idolaters.[4]

It's okay. We all do it. Idolatry is part of the brokenness inherent in the created order. God offers forgiveness. God offers the strength and means to reorient our lives in healthy ways. We just have to be aware of the issue. More, we have to be ready to speak of the issue, to acknowledge it and to hold those we love accountable. This, finally, is the crux of congregational giving. As I said earlier, giving has a way of opening us to what God might be doing, opening our posture.

If this is all true, then we must also be able to talk about the practice with others, to acknowledge our struggles, to celebrate our victories. We will not grow otherwise. Money is just another possession. In our era, it may be the most preeminent of possessions. Money represents the ability to eat, find shelter, provide care for our health, and secure our families. We convince ourselves that if we have enough, nothing can really hurt us. Even as we utter platitudes about giving being better than receiving, money not being everything, we still behave as if our financial well-being is the key to our entire well-being. As a result, we easily invest our identities in wealth. We do that as individuals and we do that as congregations. Whether individual or communal, such idolatry damages our health, distracting us from the true source of our lives and well-being.

We must address the issue intentionally, naming our distractions, calling attention to our struggles, finding our way to health

---

4. Ibid., 40–49.

with others. Suddenly, the reason we should talk about our money and generosity in a Christian community becomes clearer. Our Christian communities are supposed to be places marked by the sort of spiritual maturity in which people are able to bring their worst, in order to find their best. Scazzero's work revolves around this hope for our communities, but we have a "chicken and egg" issue. Without spiritual maturity, people won't feel safe discussing money, but discussing money is one way of expressing the sort of spiritual maturity we all desire.

It's true. At some level, we need to be mature in our conversations about money in order to become mature. Still, I have two primary practices that mark and encourage spiritual maturity in congregations. When we are part of a congregation that struggles in this sort of conversation, we might try the following: (1) discussing the pastor's knowledge of gifts from congregation members; and (2) offering testimonies about generosity.

First, hold a serious conversation about the pastor's knowledge of individual giving. Consultants always recommend this. The knowledge facilitates (1) the care for givers who may be struggling financially, or with anger with church leadership; and (2) the expression of gratitude.

Giving and receiving of care aid in solidifying a congregation's shared life. No matter how big a congregation becomes, care of members is just part of its business. Care of those who attend stitches together the fabric of the community. Sometimes, people develop situations that hinder giving to the church. Jobs are lost. Marriages come undone. Businesses fail. And yes, even good Christians sometimes get angry at the pastor or other church leaders. They often respond by withholding gifts. Sometimes, families need to. Usually, for regular and generous givers, withholding causes shame, silencing their ability to talk about what's really happening. Often, the first indication that a family is struggling consists of a couple of missed or reduced gifts. Anyone can forget a checkbook or fail to set up an online gift once. When they've been consistent in the past, then miss consistently, there's an issue. Often, only a pastor with whom they already have a relationship can make the call or visit and ask, "Is everything okay?"

It doesn't always work that well. Sometimes people evade the question. Sometimes they don't even want a trusted pastor to know. Sometimes, they simply quietly leave the church. But, more often, in my own ministry, I found that when I asked, they told me. At times, that allowed me to be a better pastor. At others, I was confronted with an expression of anger over something I'd done or some decision the church had made. I couldn't always fix those, but talking always seemed to clear the air. Once in a while, it even brought resolution and restoration of a strained relationship. Some of my biggest regrets in ministry have been times when I was too cowardly to ask a family if they were okay or angry. When I took courage, the community benefitted.

Just as importantly, if a pastor knows of individual gifts, he or she can express gratitude. Usually, only the pastor can do this. In a perfect world, people give without any expectation of gratitude. They give because they know that their money is just one expression of the way God cares for them. They give because they know that even when they give, God still cares, still provides, still preserves. They have no need to be thanked by the church or by whoever received the benefit of their generosity. But, we don't live in a perfect world.

We live in a world in which our most natural behavior is to invest our money with our identities. We live in a world in which we are skeptical that anything or anyone will help us if we let go of the one thing that makes us feel secure. We live in a world in which we know in our hearts that our fears aren't legitimate, but one in which our brains constantly scream at us to hang on to every cent we have. We live in a world in which generosity and the open posture necessary to live into God's will only comes through intentional effort and accountability. As a result, a direct, explicit, and specific expression of gratitude by someone we recognize as a leader serves as the only effective motivation for more generosity.

I don't write this as a pastor. I write as someone who gives. When a pastor thanks me for my gift, I feel great. I feel affirmed. I feel ready to try it again. When a pastor offers me thanks, it affirms a decision I made, a step I've taken in spiritual growth. That's critical for people's development, and it just can't happen unless the pastor knows what's given.

In small churches this can be painful. People expect the highest levels of privacy and have likely developed a relationship of trust with the one or two people who count the money and see the actual checks that are given. Those congregations often prefer to keep the pastor, usually an outsider, on the outside. They may love and appreciate sermons, enjoy pastoral conversations, but when it comes to money, they want the pastor to have nothing to do with their giving. In these smaller congregations, because the pastor knows everyone, the giving can provide information critical for the tailoring of care. Because of this, the small congregation is in need of spiritually mature pastors, a commodity they don't always receive, making the trust needed to share harder to give.

In large churches, this is both easier and harder. For one, the pastor is likely to have more staff working with gifts. The expectations of a larger congregation are also different. The pastor can't possibly be expected to know any but the largest givers, and will have no capacity to thank everyone for their gifts individually. In those places, staff may take on this role, especially when it comes to middle- and lower-level givers. The knowledge is likely more readily shared with pastoral staff, but the size of the congregation and the expectations of excellence are likely to be much greater.

Regardless of size, a conversation about the pastor's knowledge is critical. If a congregation doesn't already share the information with the pastor, it might talk about how that could happen. Even if a pastor already receives it, conversation about what he or she does with it can produce a great deal of benefit. The pastor might recognize a need to begin writing thank-you notes or tailoring care needs around what is learned. If those efforts are made, practices can begin that build trust and develop tight bonds between the pastor and the laity.

Second, many churches have likely considered giving testimonials. As a pastor who frequently attempted them, I can honestly say that they work great when done well, and are disastrous when done poorly. Sometimes these testimonies take the form of a leader, taking the mic in worship, speaking of how much he or she loves the church, how badly the church needs more money, and how hopeful he or she is that others will start giving in the same way. People uncomfortable with speaking in front of groups stammer around, lose their place, and confuse listeners. If you're a pastor or leader who has responsibility for worship, please, don't allow that. Don't do it to the people and don't do it to the speaker.

Talking about giving and money through testimonies in church can be powerful. But those who've not been trained to speak and developed a solid theology of generosity simply aren't equipped. They need help. Instead of just asking someone to talk about giving

99

in church, try an interview. More critically, practice the interview with the person.

After many failed attempts at creating an environment rich in congregational testimony, I started taking ten minutes of worship (all out of my sermon), setting up two tall chairs in the chancel or on the stage, and inviting a person into a conversation in front of the church. We'd rehearse it the week before. I'd start with questions like, "Why don't you share a little about your family and how long you've been coming to the church?" I'd then get specific. "One ministry in particular has made you very passionate. Could you share a little of that?" Finally, I'd turn to generosity. "You've not only been giving your time to that ministry, but you've been giving generously to the church as a whole. Could you say why you do that?" I'd end by turning it back to the congregation. "How do you think your giving is supporting God's work?" Or "What is your greatest hope for what God might do with the gifts you give?" Or even better, "How do you feel your life is better because of your generosity?"

I always had a target I wanted the person to hit, and I always helped them make sure they hit it. I didn't invent the target; the person(s) being interviewed did. Though sometimes I made suggestions. We worked out the target in rehearsal or advance conversations. I knew what they were going to say before they said it, and because of that, if they got nervous, I could help them. In those sorts of testimonial interviews, we held up miraculous transformations that had taken or were taking place. I was able to highlight amazing things that other people were doing, often without anyone else in the congregation knowing they were doing it.

When you have the resources, video works even better. Strong emotions can be evoked with music, and the kernel of a person's testimony can be distilled and presented in obvious ways. The church I last served was just on the cusp of having sufficient resources to do video well. Usually, we'd produce a quality video for special Sundays, using interviews throughout the year. In taking that strategy, we began to make people more comfortable in talking about generosity. Such talk is the beginning of the vulnerability needed for a congregation to really grow, mature, and become more generous.

Talking about money is the only way to name our edges that need growth. Small groups, open talk of finances and generosity, and healthy informal discussions can all follow testimonies, enhancing growth and leading toward greater health.

Excitement as the Building Block of Ministry

Discussion of testimonies provides a good lead-in to the next topic. I'm sure this sounds shallow, but I realized long ago that ministry was very much the practice of creating excitement. Before you express doubts, think of the Acts of the Apostles. At any given time, the apostles would preach, people would get excited, the Spirit would descend, and thousands began to follow Christ. The earliest apostles knew they had something exciting to offer.

We have good news. The lives of our churches ought to be filled with excitement. Ministry is really just tapping into it, helping people see what God is doing.

When a congregation gets excited, they have an uncanny ability to give in exceptional ways. I once watched a congregation struggling with its own finances, give a Christmas Eve offering of $40,000 for ministry in Mozambique. Why? They were excited about what was happening and felt that God was making them a part of the excitement. When people get excited, they're willing to acknowledge the power of their own generosity. When they acknowledge the power of their own generosity, they encourage and affirm their own future giving, as well as the generosity of others who may be watching. Giving begets excitement and excitement begets more giving.

Sometimes creating excitement is easy, but usually, it takes intentional effort. Once in a while, you'll have a ministry that surprises you, taking off with little or no effort. More often, pastors and church leaders must spend intentional time talking about what's next, how to create excitement around it. That practice could be its own book. Here, I'll just say this: if you want to build excitement, find a way to focus. Congregations don't always like to focus, but sometimes, too much activity can become a drain on energy. Everyone is pulled in a dozen directions, unable to find one powerful outlet. The diffusion of energy makes things feel less exciting, more mundane. I'm not saying to end every ministry in the local church. In fact, ending a ministry can add devastating complexity to the leadership task. Instead, find ways to affirm what people are doing, but gently nudge them all toward a common goal.

If the focus is to be a new children's curriculum, enlist the help of all the various constituencies. The women might prepare sets, especially if drama is involved. The men might assemble snacks. The parents of kids might be engaged in conversation about what they want for their families. Senior adults might be asked to serve as mentors or to participate in sharing with the kids. Worship can be geared around the stories being used in the first weeks of the curriculum. Most importantly, every time the pastor steps into the congregation, he or she can talk about what great things are already happening and what leadership expects next. Testimonies can be given. Prayer teams formed. The whole congregation will start to get excited as they become more involved. They may even start inviting people in the community to take part. They will start feeling the need to give financially, not just to the ministry but to the whole church. They will feel part of it all. Focus allows a congregation to hone its excitement, giving the Spirit a clear place to land and stir.

When it comes to creating excitement, pastors should also remember that nothing creates more than significantly contributing to a cause outside their local church. I've already mentioned the church that decided to make a contribution to ministry in Mozambique. That same church later made a large gift to a homeless shelter. A couple churches with which I'm familiar devote enormous Christmas Eve and Easter offerings to fresh water projects. A small church in mid-Missouri splits its Christmas Eve offering between a project to dig wells in Africa and a local ministry for children with developmental disabilities. In every case, when those gifts are made, at least when they're done effectively, the same thing happens. The congregation gets more excited, giving more than anyone expected, feeling affirmed and valued, building on the excitement for their next ministry. I often tell congregations struggling with money that the best thing they could do for themselves would be to make a public and organized offering for a ministry in their local community. Even if it means breaking the congregation's finances, such gifts are often the only thing struggling churches have left, their last chance to do something great. Sometimes, it gives them a much-needed victory, a necessary shot of energy. It may not save the church from decline and closure, but it can reorient the vision of the congregation.

Ministry is the creation of excitement. It consists of gaining a glimpse of the Holy Spirit, pointing to it, and allowing it to rush through the congregation. Ministry is about naming what God is doing, allowing people to see the power of that, fostering people's participation in it. It requires a focus on the particular place leadership has defined and a description of how the church will align itself.

Trust as the Currency for Good Ministry

The last practice I want to highlight has already been named as the result of other practices. At the same time, trust, while the fruit of good financial practices, might also be thought of as a practice in itself. Unless trust is practiced intentionally, congregations seldom display it with the consistency needed for health and maturity.

The meaning of trust can be vague. It certainly does not mean accepting all leadership decisions without question. It does not mean ignoring bad or dangerous financial practices. It does not mean turning a blind eye to poor behavior. Trust is more complex, more nuanced.

It might mean hearing a decision that one dislikes, asking questions, learning why leaders made choices they made, and then, setting aside differences to engage in ministry together. Trust might mean looking at the information shared by financial leadership, asking questions, learning how one might contribute more significantly to the financial health and wellness of the congregation, then acting accordingly. Trust might mean engaging the pastor in regular conversation, affirming him or her, and gently offering suggestions in areas in which he or she might grow. Notice I said "gently offering suggestions."

Trust most certainly does not include playing the role of a perpetual critic. It does not mean being disagreeable in meetings. It does not mean aggravating, overwhelming, or demanding things of the pastor or staff.

Trust, in a nutshell, might be thought of as the behaviors and practices exhibited by the spiritually mature. It means listening, questioning, and accepting. It means recognizing when one is taking a decision personally, when one has hurt feelings, acknowledging them to others, and working to resolve them. When congregations make intentional efforts to foster trust, to conduct themselves in trusting and trustworthy ways, they find the ability to do great work and give incredible gifts. Trust is the base ingredient for Christian community. Exhibiting it means that we must be vulnerable. We may get hurt. We may have to live with decisions we don't like. Yet, when we get it right, magically powerful generosity takes hold.

II. A Theological Approach to Congregational Generosity

All the believers were united and shared everything. They would sell pieces of property and possessions and distribute the proceeds to everyone who needed them.

—Acts 2:44-45

Acts 2:44-45 comes just after Pentecost. Many will have read it and struggled with the apparent socialism of the early Church. Americans are suspicious of sharing possessions. Yet, everything in the pragmatic side of this chapter might be found expressed here in this passage describing the early Church.

Prayer, honesty, and talk when it comes to possessions, excitement, and giving beyond the local church are all significant themes. What's more, trust underscores them all. Remember where the passage falls. The day of Pentecost descends, shaking the community, stirring them to action. The uneducated speak and the Spirit converts those who hear. The young have visions. The old dream dreams, and the day of the Lord begins. This passage I've highlighted is the response to that day.

The first disciples gathered, broke bread, shared prayers, offered their possessions for the good of the whole community, and engaged in goodness to all they encountered. The Spirit stirred and more people were added to their numbers. Notice how they aligned themselves with God's work in ways that generated excitement. Not only did many join, but the Scriptures are clear, God worked incredible signs through the apostles. The entirety of Acts is shaped by excitement for which we can only yearn. But, the passage is stitched together with this odd assertion about sharing possessions.

Why did they do that? Using the work of Luke Timothy Johnson, I've already suggested that our possessions, and money, become a wrongheaded sort of sacrament. We invest them with our selves and our self-worth. By sharing them, the first Church sought to preclude any attempt to make that investment. They insisted that the followers deal with that problem right off the bat. They had them sell possessions or bring them for the benefit of the church.

That sort of giving makes us nervous. It seems cult-like, the practice of a community in which individual identities are lost in favor of group think. That's fair. I'm not sure our churches ought to be demanding the same. But, I think we all sense that when we find ways to let go of ourselves, to shed unnecessary possessions, we find it easier to breathe, easier to connect with what God might be doing.

To get there, the first apostles had to exhibit an exceptional level of trust. This is the central theme. They so trusted each other that they committed the entirety of their possessions to the community. That took open, honest, and extremely vulnerable conversation with one another.

I'm not sure we do this as American Christians, but practices that foster trust are absolutely critical to the congregation's shared life. Without it, we will get nowhere. Without trust, without conversation, there will be no focus, no ability to align with excitement. Without trust, there will be no community that can rightly be claimed as the Body of Christ.

Theologically, generosity and openness are the sources for individual well-being. The same might be said of congregational well-being. Leaders must begin to trust, opening themselves in a wide posture, able to receive the needs of others first. Theologically, congregational finance and administration begins with generosity and the practices surrounding generosity begin and end with trust.

Chapter 6

Congregational Budgeting: Planning and Honing Ministry

Trust undergirds every practice of finance and administration in the local church. Without it, nothing works. Conflict becomes the norm. Unity is lost. Ministry fails. Once fostered and growing, however, trust leavens other practices. Budgeting is no exception.

Budgeting, as I describe it, assumes a congregation is working on its facilitation of trust. It follows the same basic pattern outlined for individual households, but because it takes place in a community, the process requires more discernment and leadership. United Methodist churches have the added complexity of a diffused committee structure. While many churches are experimenting with simplified structures, those take root only with care and attention. When embarked upon carelessly, they actually add complications. The vast majority of United Methodist churches still utilize a process in which budgeting takes place first in the Finance Committee, which refers a draft to the Church Council, a body that can amend, accept, or reject the draft. If rejected, the draft is sent back to Finance for reworking. Otherwise, whatever Church Council approves becomes the budget for the local church. At that point, leadership and, in all but the smallest churches, staff must find ways to work with the budget. Because leaders are open to interpret the budget, forced to deal with unexpected expenses, the budget becomes a living document, molded and shaped over time. At their best, they become standards for comparing actual expenses and a reporting tool for the church.

Remember: budgets are plans. They are not laws. They are not Scripture. As we'll see in the section on theological interpretation, it's not even clear that Jesus would have approved of them. Still, in our culture and age, congregations need direction and focus. They require intentionality, and a budget can be a powerful tool.

I. Practices and Patterns of Congregational Budgeting

If budgets are plans, they must be integrated into the greater planning processes of the congregation. When I was serving a local church, I led the congregation in regular planning retreats. At least annually, we'd gather and discuss what we might do next. We found powerful ways to express faith and offer opportunities for individuals. We had monthly and quarterly meetings to discuss how plans needed to shift. I had a group of five trusted leaders with whom I met weekly in an effort to keep focused. We made great strides toward building a church, but never once did I think to include the budget in that process, and that later proved costly. The budget existed as a solitary creature, one that, from time to time, would appear to bristle and even bite the hands that fed it.

When I arrived at the congregation, something just didn't sit right. There seemed to be a tension every time a leadership team picked the budget up to address it. For a while, it was fine. The Finance Team struggled with the knowledge that the general fund used to pay for most ministries had alarmingly low levels of reserves. They struggled with the knowledge that they had created and Church Council had adopted a budget with a sizable difference between planned spending and planned income. But, I was new and the church was excited. Many didn't want to think about the numbers. They just wanted to *do* ministry. I loved those people. For two years, it seemed like a good approach. We found ways to increase giving and we weren't forced to spend in some areas, meaning the planned deficit was smaller than anticipated.

Still the budgeting process took place in its own time, separate from the planning of the church's ministries. Once in a while, I'd try to accommodate additional spending needed to fund new ministries, but usually, I found it easier to ask a significant giver to add something extra. Ironically, the individuals on Finance were some of the same people engaged in the greater planning, a few even among the significant giving families I asked for additional money. Like me, they found it easier to separate the budget from the greater process.

The whole situation, shaky at times, remained tolerable until my third year. At that point, conflict escalated. It wasn't that the church fell apart. But some, especially older, more established members, began to object to certain changes. I could point a finger and criticize. I did at the time, not explicitly, not directly, but in my mind. I believed I had incorporated everyone, had engaged in an intentional discernment process with the church, had received good direction and tried to lead accordingly. Upon reflection, I realize that my process wasn't as sound as I thought.

There were other problems, but the separation of budgeting from the greater process created a source of angst, angst that ran over into other areas. More fiscally conservative members began to ask the question, "How are we paying for this?" We hadn't done anything wrong, but in the minds of many, we were playing fast and loose with a budget adopted by the leadership, and they began to say so. No one accused me or anyone else of anything illegal. Rather, they began to insert themselves in the budgeting process for the following year. That created stress in leadership teams. I knew I had a problem when the computer used by our director of youth ministry crashed. I said I'd have him one the next day. I called the treasurer and financial secretary and explained I needed to go buy a computer. Their response shocked me. "We're sorry, but that's not in the budget." I explained, as patiently as I could, that just because there was no line items labeled "youth director's new computer," didn't mean we couldn't purchase one. They suggested I call the Finance Chair. I remember thinking, *Perfect. She'll back me up. She always does.* She didn't, and in the end, I was forced to take a proposal to change the budget to Church Council. They finally approved it, essentially amending the budget, but I didn't get my youth director a computer the next day. It took two months.

The following fall, as we began to work through a new budget, things got even worse. Finance took months to develop a budget to present to Church Council, one with a new deficit, and it was rejected soundly. The process became conflicted, and that conflict began to grow. I was still generally supported as a pastor and we still did good ministry, but everything became harder. The budget became a sore spot, a place of contention, and the contention threatened to derail the ministry we were attempting. Finally, in an agonizing turn of events, the handwringing over the deficits led to a decision to significantly reduce staff positions. The staff had long needed restructuring, but without the budget to support those positions, we had to act more quickly than we wanted.

Looking back, if we'd integrated the budget into the greater planning process, we would have faced difficult staff realignments more efficiently. Hard decisions would still have been required, but might have entailed less conflict. My experience led me to the conviction that a better, more integrated budget process was needed.

Begin with Resources

As in chapter 2, everything begins with what God has given. Just as critically, a church should never separate the naming of its resources from its ministry discernment and planning processes. Ministry only begins when God gives the resources needed to conduct the ministry.

United Methodists think about vocational discernment in the same way. Everyone is uniquely gifted for some sort of ministry. One means of discerning what our particular ministry might be to name our gifts. The resources God gives provide ample evidence of the ministries to which we are called. That's true of individuals, and it's true of congregations.

Each church has a unique personality, a unique set of gifts that equip it to do some great work in the name of Jesus Christ. Finding that focus can be difficult and requires intentional planning. That said, leaders will still spin wheels and waste time unless those involved spend time thinking about and articulating the unique gifts housed in that congregation. The process too often leads to dead ends unless the people involved spend time enumerating all the gifts, including financial, brought by the congregation.

Enumerating financial gifts will include a recognition of those given in the previous year. I won't spend time justifying it, but I find the use of pledge cards helpful. Of course, if everyone just tithed, the church would have no need to receive pledge cards. But, we don't live in that sort of ideal world. People find it helpful to state what they will give and to use it as a standard. Enumerating gifts will then include a process of receiving pledge cards. That should be paired with a celebration and time of thanksgiving.

Naming the gifts will also include amounts received in the past year that had not been pledged. Naming the gifts might even include strategic plans for designated giving. Generally, state law requires that charities receiving gifts with designations must observe the designations. In my home state of Missouri, failure to follow a designation can lead to legal claims made on behalf of donors by the state attorney general. A recent case out of Mississippi even indicated that donors could force a recipient to return the gift if a designation wasn't followed.[1]

The idea of designating gifts isn't necessarily sound theologically. In a designation, the donor holds something back, namely the ability to state how the money will be used. In other words, a designated gift isn't a full gift. In a church, designations may be made for items that aren't needed. They could even enable donors to individually change the focus of the congregation. A congregation focused on creating an environment for modern worship with rock 'n roll would struggle with a donor designating a gift of $150,000 for the purchase of a new organ. Church leaders must either accept the gift and use it for an organ or simply decline it. Only the donor may change the intent. I strongly object to attempts by individuals

1. See Richard Hammar, "Liability for Ignoring Donors' Designations," in *Church Law & Tax Report*, July/August 2015: 1.

to change the collective direction of the church, and some gifts may have to be declined.

These sorts of situations have led many consultants to recommend against designations. Sometimes designations, however, are useful. I reject those developed by donors trying to change the congregation's direction. But, when designations support the direction taken by leadership, they can be used strategically to enhance a church's generosity. This is how capital campaigns work. Congregations develop a plan for a new facility and begin the process by asking leading families to make sizable designated gifts. They do so and then the total of all such gifts are shared, demonstrating a great deal of excitement, maximizing generosity. The same can be done for new ministries. Churches may deploy this strategy to dig wells in Africa or to create and implement new curriculum for children. Churches are able to remodel sanctuaries, install organs, purchase instruments and sound systems for modern worship, or launch second sites through strategically designated gifts.

During planning and discernment processes, leaders should name designated gifts as possible resources. They may incorporate plans to ask for them. Regardless, naming gifts of all varieties helps participants to recognize where their ministry ought to lead.

If the congregation operates in an economically depressed area, naming the gifts might help a congregation to be realistic about what it might do. In those same areas, people are often surprised by the extent to which they actually have the money to do what they are called to do. In other words, naming gifts has both a boundary-producing *and* boundary-extending effect on groups engaging the process.

As with individuals, groups naming a congregation's resources need to write them down in brainstorming sessions. From there, people hone what's been named, and the pastor may compare them with the patterns of giving of which he or she should be aware. Over time, everyone involved ought to have some idea of just how extensive the financial resources really are.

Counting the Costs of Ministry Focus

In this section, I want to address the costs of ministry focus, contrasting those with general costs that apply regardless of the church's ministries. That said, such a contrast is not ideal. A church should work to align every cost with its primary purpose. In the planning and discernment process, a congregation should shape itself around a single focus. "We will be the church in this community that has the best children's ministry." Or, "We will be the church in this community that works for racial reconciliation." Or, "We will be the church in this community that always seeks the next generation of Christians by reaching young adults." That focus, whatever it might be, will have associated costs, and these costs ought to be counted first.

Some consultants describe this in terms of a *missional budget*. The budget needs to reflect the mission established by the church. One ought to be able to look at the congregation's budget and know the congregation's unique call.

One may not like to admit it, but finances drive ministry. They provide a skeletal framework, and if they are shaped a certain way, doing ministry in another way may work for a while, but eventually the skeleton will shape the body. Eventually, as it did with my own congregation, friction, tension, and conflict develop. The budget must reflect the general direction of the church.

I'm not saying there isn't more to it. There must be enthusiasm for the direction leadership provides. The people must be aware and on board in order for the focus to be generally adopted, in order for finances to be adapted to it. This is why the process of budgeting, the naming of gifts, the counting of costs, must be integrated into the visioning and discernment of the church generally. One must influence the other, at all times. The resources God gives must drive ministry. The people must align those resources with their sense of what that ministry is going to be.

When the budget is assembled, the costs of ministry focus must be placed first. That isn't to say they are wholly separate from what I call the "costs of doing business," costs that will be incurred regardless of what the focus is. They can't be wholly separated because the focus ought to drive the entire ministry.

It's true that some costs are likely to be incurred regardless of what a church's focus is: building maintenance, utility costs, and staffing. Whether they should or not is a valid question. Unfortunately, churches, in another era, may not have thought about what ministry would look like in the future. They may have imposed costs on future generations, even if the ministry was forced to change. In another era, staff may have been hired or buildings built. Associated costs are often present no matter what a congregation presently believes it is called to complete. Still, they should be shaped by the congregation's current ministry if at all possible.

I recognize this is difficult, but everything listed in a budget should be touched and shaped by the current focus. Most established churches may be carrying costs from another era, costs for a building it doesn't really need or staff positions held by beloved, even gifted people, whose role isn't entirely consistent with the focus. Still, a congregation will never find its specific purpose without at least trying to align its budget.

Perhaps it's safest to simply suggest that the first costs that should be addressed and accounted for in budgeting are those associated directly with the ministry focus, while others should be evaluated against that focus. Naming the area of focus in the ministry will be critical to legitimizing it in the minds of all leaders and the church generally. The budget will be one more source of evidence for the focus itself.

Counting Other Costs of Ministry

Again, these other costs and the process of accounting for them should follow from the congregation's focus. Some costs that appear unrelated and even unnecessary might be hard to reduce or cut. Others might appear unrelated but are actually critical. For example, some leaders may imagine it possible to reduce the summer's grass cutting or winter snow removal. Given the need for hospitality for visitors, I don't recommend those decisions. The same might be said for building maintenance. When churches deal with the costs of previous eras, they often struggle to align those costs with new areas of focus. Avoiding the costs of maintenance might seem alluring, but in doing so, leaders only pass the costs for that maintenance to the next generation. Worse, deferring that maintenance exacerbates and increases future costs.

In the worst circumstances, leaders inherit older buildings the congregation always struggled to maintain, meaning that the costs of maintenance and repair often drive the process of budgeting. In established churches, leaders inherit staff structures even when they aren't consistent with the new focus. It's easy to suggest that new leadership ought to have free rein to reduce, eliminate, or change staffing, but that ignores the reality that in churches, staff are embraced as part of the fabric of the congregation. To change personnel always creates a rift.

Even with such overwhelming challenges, leaders must make an effort to align costs with the congregation's focus. They must be forthright in the conversations about those costs, at least in their planning and discernment process. In some way, they must seek to generate enough enthusiasm and excitement in order to enhance the resources they have. To use theological language, if God is calling the congregation to a new focus, God will provide sufficient resources to cover the costs of the new focus as well as the costs associated with decisions of previous generations. If God is calling the congregation to something, God will give whatever is needed, including the strength to make hard decisions, decisions including the change of staff or relocation to a new facility. The churches most successful in finding their unique call are also those who make courageous decisions about the inherited costs of a former generation.

Revisiting the Budget

Budgets require congregations to name what God is giving in order to discern future ministry. They require churches to consider the costs of their focus and to deal with costs that aren't directly related. Once that happens, budgets are developed in which every item can be traced to the focus.

As churches begin to account for their resources and costs, they must begin to compare them to the plan they developed in the budget. Again, we do not live in an ideal world. Gifts do not come in as planned. Expenses exceed or fall short of expectations. For a budget to be used effectively, it must be flexible and revisited regularly.

Conversation and revisiting of plans are simply part of what it is to lead in finance and administration. Just as churches can't be afraid to engage generosity in conversation, they must always be open to talking through their resources and expenses. I suggest at least a quarterly review of the annual budget. If it needs changing, church leaders must exhibit the courage and ability to make the necessary changes. This allows for direct and honest communication about finances. It allows for the accommodation of unexpected expenses. It forces the constant naming of resources God is providing. Even better, it becomes part of the greater evaluation of the congregation's direction, a process important for general health.

II. A Theological Approach to Congregational Budgets

When they arrived at the Lord's house in Jerusalem, some of the heads of the families brought spontaneous gifts for the rebuilding of God's house on its site.

—Ezra 2:68

In the ancient Mediterranean world, sometime around the seventh century BCE, three primary nations shaped the political landscape. Egypt, Assyria, and Babylon rose to prominence and, as all nations are apt to do, began a period of anxious coexistence. Eventually, the anxiety overwhelmed the situation and they began fighting with each other. In 605 BCE, an alliance of Egypt and Assyria attempted to defeat and repel a growing Babylon. They failed. Following its victory, Babylon slowly and methodically seized neighboring lands.

In the middle of these three powers, Israel found itself threatened on all sides. Their own telling of the story in Scripture relates the ways in which the lack of faith of their leaders led to demise.

Beginning around 592 and continuing through 586 BCE, Babylon turned its attention on Israel and Jerusalem. The city fell, the temple, the center of life and faith, collapsed, and Babylon created one of the two or three most defining moments in Jewish history.

In order to subdue conquered nations, Babylon engaged in a practice of forced exile. They destroyed a city and took its key citizens back to Babylon, resettling them, allowing them to live, but in a new location defined by Babylonian culture. They then repopulated the defeated areas with their own people. The plan worked with great effectiveness. Exiled people would settle, regardless of their angst, intermarry with Babylonians, and find themselves and their culture subsumed. The exile imposed on Israel is referred to as the "Babylonian Exile." The exile ended only when Babylon was defeated by Persia. According to the book of Ezra, the Persian king, Cyrus, then heard the petitions of the exiled Jewish leaders and allowed them to return to Jerusalem to rebuild their city and, more importantly, the temple.

Imagine living in Israel: facing a siege, suffering defeat, watching the city and temple sacked, being arrested and taken captive, and finally, relocating to Babylon, far distant from Jerusalem, and told to settle. The people settled in Babylon and lived out their lives. Only their children and grandchildren witnessed Persia's victory and received the right to return. Many would have preferred to stay in the Babylon they had known their whole lives, no matter how powerful the theology of the temple and Jerusalem might have been. Many, however, desired only to return, to rebuild.

They returned to a city without a temple or the palaces built by David and Solomon. They returned to begin from scratch. Ezra 2:68-70 relates part of the story.

I love this passage. It articulates the way communities work when shaped by God's purpose. This community, collectively traumatized by generations in exile, developed a vision. They returned and rebuilt the temple. They shaped that vision out of their sense of who God had made them to be and what their unique gifts were; and when they arrived, the first thing they did was to take an offering. In essence, their first move was to account for their resources. They established a budget out of what was offered and they began their work using those resources.

Here, we see a critical aspect of the theology behind budgets. God provides every gift that's needed to do the work set before us. We are never asked to conduct any work for which we do not have the necessary resources. If we don't have the resources to do it, we have a significant clue that God may not be calling us to that.

Throughout the New Testament, Jesus called followers to an existence shaped by a reduced dependence on their own financial resources. He called them away from careers. He called them to sell possessions. He called them to take up their own crosses, their own burdens, to follow him, to live off the kindness of strangers. That cuts against the central ideas behind financial administration. On the other hand, maybe what Jesus was really getting at was the need to recognize the source of every single resource we receive. When we rely only on the generosity and kindness of others, we come to realize that we receive only what God provides. In Acts, when the first apostles shared their possessions, they had no choice but to realize that their lives were to be shaped by the common ministry, by the path God had established, a path that lent its name to the earliest Church, The Way.

In a society shaped by financial gain, we easily lose sight of anything divine in our financial situation. We assume that we're on our own, building wealth through our own power. We must work to intentionally draw our attention and the attention of our churches back to the real source. Budgeting and incorporating that budget into the vision process assists us in doing just that.

The returning Israelites had a keen sense that God was really at work in their quest to rebuild the temple. The gifts flowed in and the thanksgiving was oriented in the right place. Not only were they reestablishing the temple, but they were seeking to reestablish their own life of faith, their own posture of openness to what God was doing.

That's what budgeting can and should do for a church. Prayers for our own generosity ought to also mark the budgeting process. The assumption of power in our work and the generation of excitement are just as inherent in building a congregation's budget. If people don't get excited talking about the budget, the plan for using God's gifts to do great redemptive and sanctifying work, then the church doesn't have the focus it needs and the congregation's vision is clouded.

Reflect on the feelings that may have been in the hearts of those seeking to rebuild the temple. I suspect they were anxious. That was quite a project after a generation of exile. More, I suspect they were convicted, and downright ecstatic that they were to be the ones, the source for God's work in the world. They poured out their gifts. They planned based on the offering. They worked and they rebuilt. What if congregations undertook such efforts in their budgets?

If we take the theological underpinnings of budgeting seriously, we must consider the role of naming God's resources, the excitement that's inherent in using them for God's work, and the focus that comes with aligning ourselves with whatever that work might be.

Chapter 7

Church Accounting: The Basics

I'm not an accountant. When it comes to writing this, I feel as if I'm stepping into the most vile of work. It isn't that I think accounting is unimportant. Instead, I feel it most vile because I feel most unqualified. When I graduated from law school, I joined a firm's corporate and securities group. There, I experienced feelings of inadequacy like never felt before, all because I didn't understand basic accounting. They don't teach accounting in law school. I cringed every time I was shown a balance sheet or financial statement. Facing the fact that I knew nothing about a subject critical to my clients' businesses played a role in driving me out of practice and into seminary. When I left the firm, I swore I'd never try to understand accounting again. I was naïve, and probably overreacting.

Even as Conference Treasurer, accounting gives me more anxiety than any other aspect of the job. I deal better with terrible church conflicts and lawsuits than I do with just the basics of accounting. In fact, "the basics" is all I feel qualified to offer. When I became Treasurer, I declared the immediate need to also hire a "real accountant," something we did and never regretted.

For these reasons, this chapter will be simplified. My hope is that pastors and leaders in local churches have felt just a bit of what

I felt when it comes to understanding church accounting. My hope is that something simple will alleviate anxiety and lead to more intentionality in church finances.

I. Practices and Patterns of Local Church Accounting

My hope is that readers recognize the logical progression from generosity to budgeting to accounting. If churches plan their ministries through budgeting, they hold themselves accountable to that plan and measure their efforts through the accounting processes. This is why, anxiety notwithstanding, I believe accounting is so important. Through accounting, local churches gain an insight that isn't otherwise possible.

Budgets are plans. Accounting practices are the means by which reports might be produced, offering leaders a glimpse of what the income and expenses of the local church look like. When done well, accounting offers a picture of how generous a congregation is becoming and the areas in which expenses are being paid. When expenses exceed plans, a conversation about why and whether spending in that area needs to continue is in order. When income falls short of expectations, a different conversation is required. Sometimes, accounting provides good news. In growing congregations, giving often exceeds the expectations. When that happens, leadership needs to be aware so it can decide what happens with the excess. When expenses fall short of expectations, leadership needs to know so that the individuals responsible might learn whether the shortfall is due to frugal practices or a failure to conduct the ministries that had been planned.

This is the purpose of accounting. To describe what practices local churches should implement, I'll discuss four areas needing intentionality: (1) how to count a dollar, (2) funds-based accounting, (3) the chart of accounts, and (4) record keeping and audits.

How to Count a Dollar

To understand local church accounting, any accounting, one must first decide how to count dollars. Believe it or not, there are two options. First, dollars might be counted only when spent or received. Accountants refer to this as *cash-basis accounting*. To best explain, suppose First UMC purchases a van for $25,000. If First UMC paid cash for the van, the accounting is easy. When $25,000 left the church's bank account and was transferred either by check, cash, or some sort of wire transfer, the church's accountant would record an expenditure of $25,000. If the administrative assistant goes to the office supply store, buys a ream of paper, and pays for it with a church check, then the expense is recorded as soon as the transaction shows up in the church's bank statement. But, what if First UMC didn't pay cash? What if they borrowed the $25,000 with a five-year financing agreement? The church would pay monthly payments of principal and interest, and those payments would continue for the next five years. Suppose the payments were $600 a month. The only expense recorded at the end of the first month in a cash-basis system would be the $600 monthly payment, even though the church actually owes $25,000 and has use of a van worth something close to the same amount.

In a cash basis system, the accounting is easy. You only count dollars spent or received. They are recorded and reported in a *statement of activities*, sometimes called an *income and expense statement* or *P & L* (i.e., profit and loss). But, such a method does not give a full picture of the local church's financial situation. Cash basis accounting provides no sense of how much debt the church might have. It offers no understanding of money expected to be paid to the church or assets it owns.

Because of the inadequacy in producing an accurate picture of an organization's finances, accountants developed a different, more accurate method known as *accrual accounting*. In accrual accounting, expenses and income are recorded when they are accrued. Expenses and income expected at a later date are classified in different categories than those already spent or received, but they are recorded. In accrual accounting, assets and debts owed are given a value and recorded on a report known as a *statement of financial position* or, in the business world, a *balance sheet*. An organization engaged in cash basis accounting can provide no statement of financial position because it has no capacity to report a debt requiring future payment or future expected income.

In accrual accounting, when an organization is entitled to receive future payments from an individual or other organization, the payments are referred to as *accounts receivable*. When an organization is obligated to make future payments but has not yet paid them, they are classified as *accounts payable*. Accrual method accounts for both, money owed to and by the church.

The organization's statement of financial position shows how much cash it has in the bank account or other sorts of financial accounts. It includes a value for any real estate or other sorts of property and adds that on a separate line. All assets are added up, including the accounts receivable. Then, liabilities or debts are added up. If the organization owes a debt to a bank that gave a loan to buy the real estate it owns or if the organization financed a vehicle or large piece of office equipment, the total amounts that are owed are totaled and then subtracted from the value of the assets, leaving a value referred to as *net assets*, the total remaining after liabilities are subtracted from assets. And yes, it is possible for that number to be negative, a situation that is not typically desirable.

Many churches use cash basis of accounting. Sometimes that makes sense. In a small church with no debt, the only income received comes from the families giving to the church. The only expenses include the amounts spent for supplies or utilities. In that case, using accrual accounting makes little sense. There's no need for the added complexity. The church doesn't need a statement of financial position or a balance sheet. Their net assets are just their assets. If they stopped operating, they would have no more expenses, and no more income. Only their building would be left with whatever the church had in the bank. In such case, the church probably doesn't need the difficult task of valuing real estate and calculating liabilities.

In mid-sized and larger churches, however, especially churches with significant levels of debt, the extra steps of accrual accounting may be absolutely critical for leaders to truly understand the financial health of the congregation. They may be receiving just enough to meet obligations, but if the debts far exceed assets, especially if the congregation had lower levels of cash in their accounts, a lost Sunday because of snow can devastate the congregation.

If a local church is in need of such methods, I strongly encourage the local church to find a volunteer or even a paid accountant. I don't mean the church needs a *Certified Public Accountant*, a title reserved for people who pass a series of exams illustrating their skill as an accountant, but the church does need someone who has engaged in professional accounting. The church needs someone who understands accrual methods.

It is also possible for an organization, including a church, to mix the two methods of accounting. Imagine a spectrum ranging from one extreme, pure cash basis, to another, pure accrual. In the middle, an organization might count most dollars on a cash basis, only when spent or received, but others when accrued. For example, a local church receiving pledges from members might not want to treat those pledges as accounts receivable. After all, members aren't obligated to pay them. They may not actually come. On the other hand, the same church, if it has a loan secured by its real estate, may want to take into account the total over the course of the year, and the total liability for the debt over its lifetime. In one area, they practice accounting on a cash basis. In the other, they use accrual. Accountants often refer to such methods in terms of *modified cash* or *modified accrual* depending where on the spectrum the accounting practices fall.

Funds-Based Accounting

In some ways, business accounting is a lot easier than that required in churches. In the business world, income typically comes from one source: customers. Regardless of the source, income is generally free for use in whatever way the owners or executives think best for business. In the nonprofit and church world, things are more complicated.

I've already identified the practice, especially prominent in churches, of designating gifts. As I indicated in chapter 6, state laws require organizations receiving designated gifts to follow the designation. Only donors may undo those designations. When someone leaves such designations in a last will and testament and dies, the organization receiving the bequest typically must follow the designation with no means of changing the donor's wishes. This means that churches and other nonprofits must create a special category of assets referred to as *permanently restricted funds*. Sometimes donors choose to temporarily restrict funds. They make a gift declaring that it must be used so long as a certain scenario exists, then freeing the funds later. At times, that might include investing the money in an investment account and not allowing its use until it reaches a certain level of return. In those cases, the funds are said to be *temporarily restricted*, but they are restricted nonetheless.

More commonly, churches create programs intended to pay for a certain ministry. Churches need new stained-glassed windows and create a window fund. They need a piano and create a piano fund. The money given for those programs are donor restricted. When it receives the gifts, the church may deposit them with the rest of the church's bank accounts, but it should account for the total given for such purpose, labeling it on the statement of financial position as a designated, permanently restricted fund. Churches that practice only strategic designations have short lists of such funds. In my experience, however, established churches that haven't been strategic have a page or more of listed funds, some with large amounts and others with just a few dollars.

This practice of fund accounting primarily occurs in nonprofit settings, especially in churches, or higher education. In those settings, donors are accustomed to making designations or targeting the income to certain expenses. General business accountants likely have knowledge of the practice, but may never have seen it at work. For this reason, a funds-based statement of financial position can be an enigma, even for experienced accountants. For now, it is enough to know that while designated funds may be placed in a general bank account, they may only be spent on the designated purpose, and should be accounted for accordingly.

Chart of Accounts

The goal of accounting is to record income and expenses in a way that makes them readily identifiable. To do this, the dollars representing particular items of income or expenses must be classified. The list of various classifications is called a *chart of accounts*, but the chart isn't just comprised of a list. Typically, the chart begins with various funds, some of which may be restricted and others unrestricted. Those funds are then broken further into a list of subcategories, and those broken into particular classifications. For example, when working with expenses, most churches will have a *general fund*, one intended for unrestricted use, intended for any expense that may need to be paid. In the chart of accounts, the general fund is usually given a number, say 1. Then, the general fund is broken into additional categories. Those categories might include pastoral compensation and lay staff salaries. They may include categories for the trustees, a classification for expenses related to the building repair and maintenance, and then for various programmatic ministries. These then get more detailed numbers (i.e., 100–199).

When creating these categories, I have two suggestions that will make administration easier throughout the year, especially for United Methodist churches. First, the categories should always take into account the budget line items as adopted by the church. This will make creating reports for leadership easier. It will also make those reports easier to read.

Second, the categories should be separated and described in accordance with any denominational reporting requirements. In The United Methodist Church, local churches must report yearly statistics to the Annual Conference statistician. Those yearly statistics are reported in three separate tables or forms, each with several different entries. One of those tables, Table II, includes various categories of expenses. If the chart of accounts and local church budget are created with that table in mind, the reporting of expenses will be much easier. Some of that reporting will necessitate a third and fourth level in the chart of accounts, each assigned a number logically corresponding to the specific level as well as the higher categories of which they are part. When a church uses accounting software like QuickBooks, PowerChurch, or Sage, the chart will take on the numbering system used by those programs, but adapted for the specifics of the local church.

Record-Keeping and Audits

Using the chart to track, a church must also be careful to keep proof of its income and expenditures. Nonprofit tax laws require it. More, churches must avoid even the appearance of improprieties or illegalities. To ensure that income and expenses are appropriate, they should retain some form of documentation, filing them in a way that makes them easy to retrieve.

To all identifiable donors of more than $250, churches must provide a letter acknowledging the gift. Copies of the acknowledgment letters should be kept and the amounts given recorded carefully.

With respect to expenses, receipts for expenditures should be kept. If individuals paid for items on behalf of the church and desire reimbursement, the church should develop a basic form including the amount requested, a description of the expense, the date made, and the person's name and address to whom the reimbursement is paid. That form should be retained along with the individual's receipt substantiating his or her payment.

Expenses will be recorded, but the records must also be retained. Those records should be kept readily available for the entire year in which the underlying payments are received or paid. After that year, or more accurately, after that year's audit, the church should retain them in a safe place, for a period of at least seven years. After seven years, the records should be appropriately destroyed to protect the personal information of anyone who may have given to the church or received reimbursement.

Payroll records might be thought of somewhat separately. In the case of payroll, the church finds itself at the intersection of its own requirements with those of the individuals receiving pay. For that reason, even more care should be taken in retaining payroll records. Because of the importance of record keeping and the need to make payments to the IRS, many churches, even mid-sized churches, retain the services of a payroll company. These companies handle all requirements and charge a fee. The payroll company will also assist with appropriate retention. Some employee records must be kept indefinitely.

As records are retained each month and entered into the general ledger, the report of those entries is then compared against the church's bank statements. All differences between what the records show and those reflected on the bank statements must be reconciled. Individuals do the same process when it comes to balancing their checkbooks. In organizations, the process is called *reconciliation* and must be done each month.

The culmination of retaining records and completing reconciliations comes with an annual audit. Each year, United Methodist churches are to provide for an audit of their financial records, a review and check of the accounting against certain basic standards. This review is to be conducted by an independent third party, meaning that nonmembers of the congregation are preferred. In The United Methodist Church, no leadership expects local churches, especially those struggling with low attendance and financial short-falls, to pay for a Certified Public Account to conduct the audit. But, every church must locate a person willing to serve as an inde-pendent, objective reviewer of the church's yearly financial records.

The audit is likely to entail a review of bank statements, the rec-onciliations completed against those statements, and a spot check of the records and receipts retained in the process. The auditor is also likely to randomly sample some of those who made financial gifts to the church, confirming that the amounts reflected in the acknowl-edgment letters and the retained records match those of the donor.

The whole process is designed with two primary purposes. First, the congregation's leadership is held accountable in their ad-ministration of the church's finances. Second, the process is meant to protect the church's resources, ensuring that dollars are spent in healthy ways and that income is received with the right sort of acknowledgment, a process of ensuring gratitude. As we transition to discuss theology, we might say that accounting and audits are means of ordering resources. They are intended to ensure that the resources given are used in the ways the congregation believes best fits God's vision for that congregation.

II. A Theological Approach to Congregational Accounting

God saw everything he had made: it was supremely good.
—Genesis 1:31

In the beginning of God's creating, nothing existed but chaos. Genesis 1 is nothing more than a description of the divine ordering of the cosmos, separating light from dark, land from sea, calling forth the creatures out of the deep, setting them in their appropriate places. Genesis 1 provides an ordered and intentional account of God's creative work.

Students of the Old Testament have likely encountered scholarly discussion of Genesis's sources, assembled over time, each with their own characteristics. A large amount of Genesis is supposed to have been the product of a "priestly" source, a writer or group of writers whose understanding of God was that of a clerical class, a class of people who had a deeply intentional and ordered understanding of creation. In the material produced by that source, God's nature is described in terms of order and purity. In such a worldview, chaos becomes the antithesis of holiness. Remaining ordered and pure becomes the ultimate goal of life in ancient Israel. Much of Leviticus with its ordered account of holy living, feeling anachronistic and odd, was produced by the same source.

We inherit this tradition and there seems to be something to it. I don't want to take the idea of order too far. There's another strain of Scripture that presents a very different worldview, one marked by a sense of the chaos and meaninglessness of life in the created world (take a look at Ecclesiastes). To get a full and developed understanding of life in this world, one probably needs a sense of both. Sometimes life needs to be ordered and intentional to ensure satisfaction. At other times, we simply cannot control the chaos and are best served allowing it to swirl, waiting for a glimpse of God in the midst of the movement.

When it comes to finance and administration, I speak from experience: the ordered life is better. In finance and administration, holiness is marked by intentionality and purpose in every action we take. This is the nature of church accounting.

This isn't easy for me to write. I find myself fascinated and inspired by a little chaos. I like the things of this world that can't quite be captured with words or numbers. I offer art, poetry, and music. These are activities that deal in the creative, in the chaos of the Spirit, in inspiration that can't be reduced to something we can really perceive. They work in the chaotic realm of our emotions and feelings, tapping into some sort of chaotic soul of creation. In Ecclesiastes, the author matter-of-factly describes our attempts to control the world around us, as the "vanity of vanities" or more accurately, as "vapor," something impossible to grasp. With the author of Ecclesiastes, I want to throw up my hands and insist that the only things to do are to eat, drink, and be merry. But, such an approach in finance and administration, at least at some level, is just going to generate trouble.

Maybe we should reconsider this bifurcated approach to understanding the world. Maybe the world is at once chaotic and ordered. Maybe the creative process of bringing order can actually assist us in living with the chaos. Even creative activities, those that aren't easily reduced to words and numbers, carry an order with them. The order, the form around those things, is what makes them perceptible. Music, in reality, can be understood as a form of mathematics, each note consisting of an event in time, and characterized by the length of sound wave needed to produce it. Poetry, even in free verse, is marked by rhythm, consisting of words occurring in time and space on the page. Consistent with Genesis 1, all of life has an order, a place, a time, a rhythm.

Accounting provides order, making something as imperceptible as the inspiration behind a poem or piece of music, easier to understand. Many of my colleagues are frustrated by the difficulty in measuring the success of a congregation. I'll admit, spiritual growth and maturity aren't exactly things that can be reduced to numbers. Neither is the health and vitality of a local church. We can certainly say that a church that is rapidly losing attendance is most likely a church that isn't well. But there are times when even growth in attendance numbers may be undergirded by theology and attitudes that are more dysfunctional than healthy. The truth is, it's hard to talk about what vitality really is. Any one measure is far from sufficient to give leaders a full picture of what's really happening. The vitality and maturity of a congregation, a collective spirit of a congregation, is part and parcel of the underlying soul in the world, a soul always present, always seeking expression. What if we imagined accounting, something I for one have never particularly found interesting, as one more form we might use to express what is otherwise inexpressible?

Behind the numbers, we start seeing things like the generosity of a community. We gain a glimpse of the focus and direction of a congregation's spending. We separate income from expenses, dollars used for staff from those used for maintenance. We see how the congregation is using its money and we can compare it to the words of the pastor and leadership when they articulate the direction for the church's future. Using the reports that accounting makes possible, we can actually glimpse what's happening with an enormous aspect of congregational life; and for that reason, we must be careful, intentional, and as ordered as we can possibly be.

Chapter 8

Legal Matters: Maximizing a Congregation's Resources for Ministry

Whether we like them or not, we must make an intentional effort to address finance and administration. This is true in our individual and congregational lives.

Healthy and holy living runs in two directions. Individuals who "become more vile," making the effort to better manage individual finances, will be better equipped to lead congregations making the same sorts of efforts in community. Congregations with healthy administrative practices offer formative instruction for individuals seeking financial health for themselves and their families.

It seems that our language automatically employs metaphors of physical health. We speak of "healthy living," "wholeness," and "well-being" when it comes to finances.

I'll take this further. I've discussed matters we might describe as the muscular and skeletal systems of individual and congregational life. In personal life, generosity, budgets, retirement savings, and taxes form a constellation of absolutely essential practices needed to support or uphold everyday activities. In congregations, generosity, budgets, and accounting provide the same critical shape and support for the congregation. Without good practices, the congregation will collapse. These practices structure and support everything a congregation does.

Other administrative matters operate to enhance or protect a person or congregation's health. These work more like an immune system, and neglecting them leaves a hole in congregational health. I'm opting to include four such issues in this final chapter, all of which have a legal dimension: congregational taxes, building use, intellectual property, and vendor contracts.

I. Practices and Patterns of Basic Church Legal Matters

All four of these areas are more complicated and significant than described here. Consider this chapter an introduction and warning. All four areas—taxes, building use, intellectual property, and contractual relationships—affect nearly every established church, enhancing or degrading ministries. Intentionally addressing them will offer a valuable insulation against conflict and interference. Neglecting them will require resource-wasting attention.

Congregational Taxes

Wait. Congregations don't pay taxes. Right? I only wish. As I said in chapter 4, some taxes owed to the federal government lie at a complicated intersection of obligations of the congregation, its employees, and those who support it with their gifts. At that intersection, churches suffer confusion, stress, and in the worst scenarios, conflict, especially when the Internal Revenue Service is involved. Few things elicit a more visceral and negative response from church leaders than a letter from the IRS, and I'm asked more tax questions than any other variety. Richard Hammar has made a significant career producing an annual volume on clergy and church tax.[1] This single section is in no way meant to replace or even compete with Hammar. In fact, in my work, I regularly consult his guide and newsletter. My intention here is to provide a short and concise description of a small number of issues about which I'm asked, especially in United Methodist contexts. As with clergy, if a church leader has an issue related to taxes, he or she should turn to a tax professional. If a church leader wants to know more about taxes affecting congregations and clergy, I recommend Hammar's book and newsletter.

The questions I get most often when it comes to taxes fall into three major categories: nonprofit status, payroll taxes, and state/local taxes.

(1) Nonprofit Status

The question with which I started this section is apt. Churches don't pay taxes, right? That's true of federal income tax. Most organizations, especially businesses, are required to pay a complicated web of taxes based on income. Churches and other nonprofits, however, are exempt. The tax code provides this exemption to organizations existing for certain purposes. The Internal Revenue Code labels one such category "religious."[2] An organization that exists for *religious* purposes may be exempt. Churches fit that description.

---

1. See Richard Hammar, *2015 Church & Clergy Tax Guide* (Carol Stream: Christianity Today, 2015).
2. 26 U.S.C. §501(c)(3).

Unfortunately, the tax code is never as easy as that. In addition to tax-exempt status, charitable organizations are also entitled to receive tax-deductible gifts. In other words, organizations organized for exempt purposes may also receive donations, and those who give the donations are then entitled to reduce their taxable income by whatever they gave to that organization, as discussed in chapter 4. In some way, then, the US government offers charitable organizations two forms of tax relief. They do not tax income received by the organization, and they allow individuals to shield amounts donated. This combination of exemption and deduction provides enormous relief to charities, as well as, while it may be debated, at least some incentive to individuals to support those charities.

At the same time, the exemption and deduction cost the US government revenue they would otherwise receive. Because of that, while the exemptions and deductions are automatically given, the IRS does seek to protect itself and the United States from fraudulent practices. To do that, it has developed a system by which organizations may, even must, obtain a determination from the IRS that the purpose of the organization is exempt and that gifts are tax deductible. Typically, the process first involves identifying one's organization with the IRS. Every organization or business, at least those with any employees or desiring some sort of status with the IRS, must apply for an identification number, obtained with a form called an *SS-4*. The identification number, called a *Federal Employer Identification Number* or FEIN, is used to identify every organization, for-profit or nonprofit, by the IRS and other governmental agencies. Think of them as Social Security numbers for businesses.

The SS-4 is simple, taking up less than one page. It can even be completed online at www.irs.gov or faxed, with a response typically arriving in twenty-four hours. If a church is established, it likely already has a FEIN. If it does, my advice is simple: don't share it with other organizations and don't lose it.

After obtaining the FEIN, an organization desiring recognition as a tax-exempt organization entitled to receive tax-deductible gifts may apply for a 501(c)(3) determination. This is done through a longer, more complicated form called a *Form 1023*. The Form 1023 requires a narrative of the organization's purpose as well as three years' worth of financial data or, for new organizations, three years of projected financials or budgets. Often a Form 1023 will require the assistance of an attorney or accountant, especially in stating the organization's purpose in a way the IRS will accept. Once the IRS grants approval, it issues a *determination letter* to the organization, a letter that, like the FEIN, should be kept safe and only shared with donors wanting proof of the deductibility of their gifts. Following the determination, while the organization is not required to pay taxes, it must file returns or reports with the IRS on an annual basis. These returns are provided on yet another form called a *Form 990*. The 990 isn't particularly difficult, but they do require financial reporting best undertaken by an accountant.

This is how it's typically done. For United Methodist churches, however, the process, at least for now, is simpler. For the last few decades, the IRS has allowed large organizations with many chapters to obtain *group letter rulings*. Such group rulings were created for organizations just like The United Methodist Church, organizations with fairly sophisticated, overarching structures, but with chapters or local outlets that may or may not have the resources to provide the IRS with complicated returns and reports. In The UMC, the group letter ruling was obtained by the General Council on Finance and Administration (GCFA), one of The UMC's general agencies with responsibility for resourcing annual conferences, local churches, and other United Methodist organizations in matters of finance and administration. The group letter ruling allows every United Methodist local church, at least those that have been recognized by GCFA, to claim tax-exempt status and receive deductible gifts. At least for now, it also entitles every local church to avoid the complication of filing a Form 990.[3] Assuming a church is recognized by GCFA, occurring through application with GCFA and the annual conference of which the church is a part, a local UMC is automatically included in the group letter ruling.

I want to offer a warning with respect to tax-exempt status and the deductibility of donations. There are behaviors for which the IRS will revoke a church's status. The two most prominent or riskiest are political activities and what is known as *private inurement*. With respect to the political activities, churches have broad, far-reaching protections under the First Amendment of the Constitution. As such, the pastor may advocate for any cause he or she believes consistent with the gospel. However, the tax code does not allow any organization that supports particular candidates for office to obtain tax-exempt status, at least as a religious organization under 501(c)(3). Thus, if a pastor turns from advocating for a cause to advocating for particular candidates on behalf of the church, he or she puts the church's tax-exempt status at risk. It doesn't matter on which end of the political spectrum the pastor falls. Any official advocacy of candidates for office or even of a particular political party may lead to a revocation.

Second, if an organization obtains recognition under 501(c) (3), no benefit from the organization may *inure* to a private indi-

---

3. The IRS has indicated it may continue with group letter rulings but begin requiring local chapters and churches to file individual Form 990s at some point in the future. If this occurs, then local churches will require better accounting and reporting than they have previously had.

vidual or entity. In other words, the organization is free to support its charitable purpose through distributions and expenditures of money. It may provide donations to other charitable organizations. But, the organization may not provide gifts or contributions to private individuals, unless they are somehow benevolent recipients per the organization's charitable purpose. Distributions might be made for scholarships or certain grants, but no donor may designate them for the benefit of a particular individual. Likewise, no individual may receive a tax deduction for gifts given or directed to private individuals. This comes up in local churches when the congregation desires to support a particular individual or family. Members are more than welcome to pool their money and make a gift to such a family, but the gifts they give are in no way tax deductible. Congregations occasionally seek to make generous gifts to pastors or other staff. Again, such gifts are fine, but they must be treated as part of the employee's compensation, requiring their own payment of income and payroll taxes. If that doesn't happen, if churches simply give gifts for which they do not provide evidence and require the individuals to recognize them as income, the IRS may levy penalties against all parties involved, including revocation of tax-exempt status.

Finally, once an organization obtains recognition by the IRS, in order to preserve the deductibility of donations, the organization must provide donors with an acknowledgment of gifts. This is often done through an acknowledgment letter or through giving statements issued to regular givers. Such documentation must be provided to donors giving more than $250 per donation, whether in cash or through in-kind gifts. For donors who give such gifts regularly, a phenomenon common in churches, the organization may simply provide an annual statement of every gift made. The statement or acknowledgment letter must include, at a minimum, the following:

1. The name of the organization

2. The amount of contribution or description of non-cash contributions and their value

3. A statement that no goods or services were provided in exchange for the gift and/or the only benefit received in exchange for the gift was an intangible religious benefit

If the statement fails to meet these requirements, the donor may not use it to support a tax deduction. In fact, some significant donors have lost the deduction when the local church failed to include the sentence stating that "no goods or services were provided in exchange for the donations, other than intangible religious benefits."

The IRS considers the receipt of such acknowledgments to be the sole responsibility of the donor. In other words, churches that fail to provide them are not at risk for criminal or civil penalties from the IRS. Instead, they are at risk of angering givers who lose large deductions for gifts given. For that reason, churches should make every effort to get their giving statements and gift acknowledgments right.

(2) Payroll Taxes

As I describe in chapter 4, churches must pay Medicare and Social Security taxes for non-clergy staff. In addition, churches must report income paid to employees (clergy included), as well as anything paid to organizations and individuals in exchange for services rendered as independent contractors.

With respect to Medicare and Social Security, churches must withhold 7.65 percent from amounts paid to employees, other than clergy. This 7.65 percent represents the amounts owed for a particular individual's Medicare tax and the Federal Insurance Contributions Act (FICA) contribution. The church must then match the 7.65 percent and pay the entire amount (15.3 percent of the compensation) to the IRS, with a quarterly return known as a *Form 941*. Employers often utilize payroll companies to pay employees, file payroll taxes, and issue the required reports. As I've already indicated, employers of clergy are not required to withhold payroll taxes, and many payroll companies may be confused by this, making it necessary to locate one that understands the complications of paying staff mixed with laity and clergy.

In addition to withholding payroll taxes, employers are required to withhold a certain amount from individual compensation to offset the income tax that individuals will be required to pay. Again, this requirement does not apply to clergy in religious employment. All of these amounts, payroll tax and withholdings for income tax, are determined by the employee's completion of a *Form W-4*, a form the employer must retain with proof of US citizenship or authorization for employment of residents from other countries. Again, because of how complex the withholding process becomes, I strongly advise even small or medium-size churches to assume the cost of contracting with a payroll company.

Withholding and record retention is only part of the issue. At the end of each year, no later than January 30, an employer must report to employees, their income for the year. The report is issued on a form that most individuals have received, the W-2. Churches should especially note that even though they aren't required to withhold either payroll taxes or income tax for clergy, they must nonetheless issue a W-2, just as if they were a lay employee. Beginning in 2016, large churches sponsoring a health insurance plan may also have been required to file new forms with the IRS and to provide an additional report to employees. These new forms, 1095-B and 1095-C, only add complexity to the reporting requirements. One can see why I strongly advise locating a payroll company.

In addition to employee reporting, churches may be obligated to issue certain tax reporting forms to other non-employee individuals and businesses who were contracted for services. These forms, known as *1099s*, report non-payroll distributions of money to any person or business. Churches that do not hire an employee to clean the church, but which engage the services of a cleaning company, will be required to issue a 1099 to the cleaning company. Churches that engage a window washer to annually wash the windows would do the same thing. The same goes for recipients of scholarships or grants from a local church.

Church leaders often get confused whether an individual was engaged under a contract for services or hired as an employee. Churches get especially confused when it comes to musicians, nursery workers, and providers of custodial services. The IRS generally looks at specific facts and circumstances to decide whether someone is to receive a W-2 or a 1099. Generally, if an individual is free to set his or her own hours, brings his or her own supplies, and has a set duration in which to finish the work, he or she should be treated as a contractor, requiring a 1099. Those individuals hired and directed by church leadership in how they do their work, provided with the supplies needed to do the job, and who work consistently over the course of a long duration will be treated as employees requiring a W-2 and all payroll withholdings. In my experience, nursery workers who must show up for worship services, use supplies provided by the church, and are directed under a local church's policies are employees. The same goes for those cleaning the church. Meanwhile, if an individual provides cleaning services, brings in his or her own equipment and supplies, and is allowed to set a schedule in conversation with church leadership, the relationship is likely of a contractual nature requiring a 1099.

(3) State/Local Taxes

Finally, a section on congregational tax wouldn't be complete without at least some mention of state and local tax issues. Some states, Missouri for instance, require an income tax similar to that of the federal system. In those states, they typically allow organizations exempt from federal tax to also avoid state income tax. Each state will be different. Some states impose a sales tax upon retailers, who charge the tax to customers. In those states, charitable organizations are often allowed to obtain an exemption from sales taxes. This usually entails filing a form and receiving an acknowledgment letter. Finally, many municipalities and/or counties impose a tax on the assessed value of real estate. Usually, those municipalities recognize that churches have some claim for exemption from such taxation under the First Amendment of the US Constitution. As such, they may file to exempt the real estate used. However, in many cases, property simply held for investment will not be treated as exempt, requiring churches to pay taxes on any sort of property they own and lease to tenants or even vacant property held for some future use. My only purpose here is to identify the issue and to suggest that churches should be aware of the taxes they may be obligated to pay or from which they may request exemptions.

Building Use

Taxes aren't the only matters requiring attention. Except in rare instances and in the case of new church starts, most established churches in the United States own a building used for its ministries. Buildings provide a resource and a responsibility for congregational leadership. When it comes to insulating a church from issues relating to the building, a congregation must make an intentional effort to structure building use in healthy ways, especially for outside organizations and individuals.

First, building use of any sort, whether by the local church's ministries or other individuals and organizations, must be insured. Insurance policies, expensive as they are, are absolutely critical to the safe and responsible operation of a church building. No matter how small a congregation, failing to provide adequate insurance is simply unacceptable. Insurance must be obtained to (1) protect individuals against losses related to their own physical or emotional injuries, insurance known as *general liability* insurance and (2) protect against losses the congregation may suffer as a result of damage to or destruction of the building itself, insurance known as *property and casualty* insurance. There are many more forms of insurance a church needs (i.e., worker's compensation and director and officer coverage), but these two forms relate most directly to building use. General liability coverage will protect the church if a guest slips and falls, incurring injury. The second form insures compensation in the event of fire or storm damage.

Individuals and organizations pay a fee to an insurance company called a *premium*. In exchange, the insurance company issues a "policy," naming the sorts of losses it will pay for if incurred. Assuming the individual or organization never incurs a loss, the company is never obligated to render a benefit or pay out for damages.

If, however, a loss is incurred, at least assuming it is named as a *covered loss* in the policy, the insurance company will make the necessary payments to compensate. Churches might have conversations about the amount of coverage they need on a building, especially if they occupy a building too large for their current community. But, some property coverage, and significant coverage for liability insurance, are critical. I know of very few churches that haven't incurred some loss, whether for hail damage to the roof, loss associated with a fire, or claims from individuals who suffered physical injury while attending a church event.

Churches must have insurance, but when it comes to allowing non–church-related entities to use the building, congregations must take an additional step. I'll be the first to advocate for allowing community groups to use church buildings. Part of being a witness to the good news is providing a presence and resource for the surrounding community. On the other hand, such use can create confusion, especially when use leads to injury or conflict within the church. For that reason, I also advocate the development of well-written, clear, and concise building policies that outside groups must follow. Non–church-related organizations and individuals should sign a *building use agreement* or a *lease* for space in the church's building. A building use agreement is appropriate for general use of the church's building, especially for one-time or limited reoccurring events. A lease is appropriate to allow full occupancy of a particular space in the church's building.

These documents should be developed by church leaders in consultation with an attorney who understands the particular needs and decision-making structure of the local church. The attorney should understand how United Methodist churches hold ownership to their buildings (i.e., in trust for the Annual Conference) before

149

drafting any lease agreement for extended occupancy. Still, these documents are absolutely necessary to prevent misunderstandings and to allow a congregation to maximize its resources.

The terms of a lease will certainly differ from that of a building use agreement. For one, a lease will describe a basic area that a tenant is entitled to occupy, an area that the church, as landlord, may enter, but which must be preserved so that the tenant may use it undisturbed. A building use agreement will simply state the scope of use in which a person or organization may engage. That said, both documents should be very clear with respect to the following:

1. the permitted uses, clearly defining the scope of the agreement

2. the term or duration, whether a longer lease term or a shorter use

3. the amount of any money the user or tenant must pay to the church, and when the amount is due

4. that the user or tenant will carry its own insurance and agrees to defend the church from liabilities arising from the use or occupancy

This may seem excessive to smaller churches, but liabilities and claims that arise out of building use can be devastating. To do the ministry to which it is called, a church may need to accept a use that carries high risks. For example, a church may agree to host a homeless or feeding ministry. Churches may decide to host senior ministries or work with people with developmental disabilities. Such uses are consistent with a church's mission to reach people with the gospel, but they carry with them risks to vulnerable populations. I suggest that a church be clear about the nature of the relationship created with an organization or individual conducting such ministries. It must, while offering use of a valuable resource, also protect that resource for its use with other ministries. A church that incurs a debilitating loss associated with building use will not be able to adequately conduct other ministries to which it may be called.

As a final word on building use, I should mention that churches receiving income from building use or rentals should be cautious about the tax status of that income. The Internal Revenue Code contains a provision under which the IRS may impose a tax for income received by a charity from business unrelated to that charity's charitable purpose. For churches, this means that rent might be subject to this tax, called the *Unrelated Business Income Tax* ("UBIT"). Fortunately, most such income from rents associated with the church building or even a home owned by the church do not trigger the UBIT. However, UBIT applies when a church receives rent from a building on which it has incurred debt, say a mortgage on a home or building. For this reason, the receipt of such income should trigger a conversation with the church's legal and accounting professionals to ensure the income does not incur unwanted tax.

Intellectual Property

Not all property owned by a church involves land, buildings, or the stuff in the building. Some property can't be described in physical terms. Instead, it's held in the minds of church leaders or in the digital memories of a church's computers. In the digital age, churches must better understand this sort of property, as they will be finding themselves in more disputes or difficult situations related to *intellectual property* than ever.

Difficult situations typically relate to one of two categories of intellectual property. One sort of intellectual property relates to ideas. Every ministry begins with an idea. Churches develop ideas with respect to their identity and the words or images used to express it. In The United Methodist Church, GCFA, the same agency that holds the IRS's determination letter, also owns all the intellectual property associated with the famous "flame and cross" of The United Methodist Church. GCFA allows all local churches to use that logo, but they restrict the means by which churches do so. Other examples include curriculum developed by a church leader. Even this book is an asset of intellectual property. Lawyers have terms to classify different forms of intellectual property. They speak of trademarks, copyrights, and patents. United States law treats each one differently, and churches may end up with issues in any of those categories, especially trademarks and copyrights.

The terms relating to intellectual property are less important than understanding a few basic concepts. For example, the owner of an asset of intellectual property is usually the person who developed the idea in the first place. Unless circumstances dictate otherwise, an author of a book is the initial owner of that book, a *copyright*. The designer who creates a logo is the owner of the logo, a *trademark*. The inventor of an invention owns the idea behind the invention, a *patent*. The US government has developed a process of registration by which individuals and organizations owning such property may put everyone else on legal notice of their ownership.

Often, however, the property is transferred to some owner other than the creator. In the case of written work, a publisher ends up with the copyright, paying the author a share of any money it makes on the sale of the book. In the case of a trademark, the designer may transfer it to the organization for which it was designed.

To make matters more complicated, if an individual creates a work as part of his or her employment, the employer actually owns the intellectual property. This will be important as we begin to discuss how churches might be affected.

Church leaders and staff must always remember that ideas, pictures, written works, movies, music, software, and other data are pieces of intellectual property, and the church must obtain permission from the owner of the property in order to use them. When churches or leaders fail to obtain appropriate permission, they often end up in trouble. I'll offer a few examples.

First, churches are suffering from more legal claims associated with the use of photographs or other design graphics. The claims usually arise when a well-intentioned church leader searches the Internet for a picture or graphic. They locate one, fail to recognize it as the intellectual property of another organization, and put it to use in bulletins, in newsletters, or on websites. They later receive a letter from the owner, demanding payment for the use, usually with a threat of litigation. Many of these letters, while somewhat grounded in the law, are the product of companies seeking out just such unauthorized use. They reduce the visibility of their copyright or trademark claims, making individuals believe they need no permission. They track use of the picture or graphic using software, *trolling* the Internet for possible claims. This is nefarious, but a practice of which churches must be wary.

The best practice to avoid these sorts of claims is to simply avoid using any picture for which clear permission of the owner is not given. Churches may use a photo or graphic service to do this. Some are even free, while others charge a nominal fee for access to large quantities of images. Services specializing in high-quality, high-resolution images may be more expensive. Still, these services, at least reputable ones, offer assurance of all the appropriate permissions necessary to use the images they offer (referred to as *licensing*).

Second, church leaders often fail to realize that music is owned by the artist who created it or by the publisher who produced it. As such, when a congregation sings a song in worship, it requires permission. For music found in the hymnals of denominations, including The United Methodist Church, the permission is granted through the purchase of the hymnals. For other music, however, permission must be sought from the owner of the intellectual property. Services have developed that ensure the appropriate licensing for music. However, those services require payment as well as careful record-keeping when it comes to what music was used when.

For a list of examples of licensing services, see my website www.nateberneking.com.

Third, churches often fail to realize that a person's likeness or image is, itself, a form of intellectual property. Most people appreciate the use of photographs taken by church members of each other in worship, whether online or in printed materials. That said, the use of such images requires the permission of the person captured in the image. This becomes especially sensitive with respect to children, whose parents or guardians must give permission on their behalf. There are exceptions to this rule, but to comply with all legal requirements, churches should obtain a written agreement for use. That may seem excessive, but at a minimum, churches should obtain written permission from the parents of children. I am aware of several anecdotes involving churches that developed uncomfortable situations after publishing photos of children. They might even be endangered by it. Unfortunately, these situations have become easy to create in an age of social media.

Finally, churches occasionally develop disputes with staff around programs or curriculum, especially when the staff person desires to publish the work for sale. While facts and circumstances vary, work created by staff in the scope of employment, belongs solely to the employer. If the employee later desires to publish something created in the scope of work, he or she will need permission from the church. The employee isn't allowed to register copyrights or trademarks in his or her individual name when this is done. Difficult situations are often the result of the employee's misunderstanding. When creating such materials in the church, it may be helpful to have conversations about ownership, use, and employment terms up front. At times, it may even make sense to develop appropriate written agreements.

Another growing area of concern relates to the data churches retain. Churches retain a host of data with respect to the people who attend. They keep names, addresses, birthdates, phone numbers, and even financial information related to the amounts an individual person or family gives to the church. The increased incidence of identity theft and data breaches have led the United States and many states to develop laws around the protection of such data. Churches are often exempt, but this doesn't mean they are exempt from the negative consequences and loss of trust associated with a data breach. In fact, churches should work very hard to secure their data through a reputable Internet technology provider, while also working to develop a plan of action in the event of data breach or loss. Such plans usually entail a plan for communication and the efforts that will be undertaken to restore trust (i.e., free credit monitoring for victims).

Vendor Contracts

As a final area of concern, churches need to read and review any contracts the church has with various vendors. Yes, church leaders should read these contracts. As someone who once drafted them, I can say that few tasks are more vile. This sort of work requires a committed person. Unfortunately, many of the salespeople using these contracts with customers haven't read them either. A great deal of confusion develops when churches enter them without an understanding of the basic terms governing a relationship with a vendor.

The most common sorts of contracts include office equipment leases, especially copiers, cleaning contracts, pest control agreements, and service agreements relating to computers or other equipment (i.e., heating, ventilation, and air conditioning). Most churches will not be able to hire an attorney to review agreements that aren't likely negotiable anyway. Most vendors will simply not provide the goods or services subject to the contract if a church is unwilling to sign on the terms as presented. These agreements should at least be read, reading that will ensure the church is able and willing to comply.

Reading contracts is not enjoyable. I suggest a guided reading. Any church leader or pastor preparing to sign such a vendor contract should read to answer the following questions:

1. How long does the agreement last and will it renew automatically?

2. When are payments due and what are the terms?

3. Under what circumstances must the vendor provide services?

4. When may the church cancel the agreement, and under what terms?

5. What happens in the event of a dispute?

6. What other responsibilities does the contract impose?

For every agreement, some devoted leader should review the contract and provide a summary of those answers. A spreadsheet might be created with termination dates and automatic renewals. This sort of hard work allows church leadership to better strategize around future relationships with vendors.

When churches aren't aware of the answers to these six questions, disputes almost certainly arise. Many churches enter into leases for copiers. Doing so prevents the church from having to purchase a large piece of office equipment it may not be able to afford. These leases can be especially helpful when requiring equipment that becomes obsolete or loses value quickly. The vendor is almost always willing to replace a copier more than a few years old if the church is willing to renew for another lengthy term (often five years). On the other hand, churches find themselves in trouble when they are less than satisfied with a piece of equipment after two or three years and wish to change vendors or find themselves able to purchase a new piece of equipment at a cost less than the current lease payments. In those instances, when a church enters an agreement without knowing the terms, leaders find themselves wanting to cancel but having no way to do so under the terms of the contract. Some vendors aggressively refuse cancellation, even refusing to retrieve the equipment until the lease term is complete.

When churches enter without a good sense of basic terms, leaders end up with inadequate services or constant aggravation trying to schedule services. They end up paying more than they should for repairs, all because they entered an agreement they believed would make life easier.

I'm not opposed to vendor contracts. They often provide high levels of savings and support that a church might not otherwise find. But churches should always understand both the agreements they have already signed and any new contracts before entering them. Often those agreements may relate to each other.

All of these practices might be thought of as means of ensuring the best use of congregational resources. They won't be the means of producing great fruit for ministry. They will not attract large numbers of people. But, without them, the church is almost certain to flounder, to end up in conflict and to reduce the effectiveness of its ministry. Practices around basic matters of law and administration allow a church to engage in ministry, obtaining the most value out of its resources. These practices, vile though they are, simply comprise the basic costs of doing effective ministry. More, I believe they are supported by, even as they also influence and form, a theology that grounds this entire work.

II. A Theological Approach to General Legal and Administrative Matters

The kingdom of heaven is like a man who was leaving on a trip. He called his servants and handed his possessions over to them. To one he gave five valuable coins, and to another he gave two, and to another he gave one.

—Matthew 25:14-15

In the parable of the valuable coins, known more commonly from older translations as the parable of the talents, the master only condemns the servant who failed to put his coin to any use at all. The only sin earning a servant condemnation seemed to be one of omission. The amount of return was largely irrelevant. One servant clearly made the best use, but he received no more affirmation than the one who tried but received a smaller return. The servant who simply buried his coin, however, is the servant who earned the outer darkness.

When it comes to the Christian life, individual or communal, we sometimes find it easiest to stop trying. Fear or despair sets in, we throw up our hands, and we refuse to make an investment in ministry. We end our small groups, lay out of worship, withhold our finances, and cease our prayer or devotional practices. Churches ignore building maintenance, scale back evangelism activities, end talk about personal finances and generosity, and forget even the most basic of hospitality. Individuals develop the idea that they have nothing to offer, and so, don't. Congregations end any effort to inventory their resources. They lose the connection between that inventory and the ministries to which they might be called. They lose track of mission and enter a phase of going through the motions, of empty activities they do only because the rhythm of doing them brings some sense of comfort, nostalgia, or peace of mind. I have a hard time even seeing the Church in such congregations. Burying coins, ending effort, calling it quits—this is the great sin Jesus describes in his parable. Committing to the kingdom of God, aligning self to God's work, taking the open posture with which I started, requires an effort, an investment.

There's more. Perhaps burying a coin isn't just an analogy to the failure to engage in ministry. It might be read more subtly, implicating us when we fail in intentionality. When I read the parable I see multiple layers of meaning. Upon reading it the first time, I saw a servant frozen with anxiety and fear. He who buried his coin presumably sought to preserve it. He buried it in order not to lose it, fearing that its loss might incur an angry response from the master. As it turned out, in a twist of irony, his fear drove him to the very sort of protectionist practice that did anger the master. On a second read, however, I saw a servant who, imagining he was preserving his coin, failed to consider the possibilities for investment with any intentionality whatsoever. With no thought, the easiest means of acting was to ensure the coin's protection. He never gave the coin a second thought. The other servants actually put thought into their investments and the result was a return, bigger or smaller, but a return nonetheless.

At once the parable warns against fearful paralysis and the risks of unintentionality. Temptation pulls local churches in two directions. In one, churches find themselves the victims of fear, turning in on themselves, taking action not to reach new disciples, but to protect what they have, burying their ministry behind their building, organ, piano, choir, worship style, endowment, kitchen, pews, pulpit, or stained glass. Turning dour, they sit through decelerating worship experiences, searching for that which makes them comfortable, drawing on the generosity of a previous generation, searching for ways to continue paying the costs incurred by those same past people. Comfort, nostalgia, peace of mind, lack of risk characterize their attendance at *their* church. In the other direction, leaders—desperate to grow, to locate more people, to raise more money—lose their ability to think carefully. They take risks, building buildings that never should be built, changing worship times in hard-fought and confusing conflicts, spending money on the next program, all the while, loosely accounting for finances, refusing to think about the accountability of staff and ministry leaders.

In one direction, churches fall victim to the wrong sort of intentionality, one shaped by protectionism. They bury their coin, fearing its loss. In the other direction, churches act with no thought whatsoever. Maybe they don't bury their coin, so much as they lose it in the dirt. The point is, they take the easiest, the most glamorous, the least resistance-producing paths in ministry. In either case, the coin is lost. In either case, financial and administrative practices become a hindrance. Worse, many churches fall victim to both sorts of temptation at once. They constantly battle demands grounded in nostalgia, comfort, and peace, meaning that their activities and energies are directed at protecting what the church has always had. At the same time, their despair and desperation leads them to carelessness, spending where they need not or ought not spend, conducting themselves without thinking through what they are doing.

"The Holy Spirit never precluded good planning." I'm forever grateful for that advice. It is true in worship, and it is true in finance and administration. Leadership requires intentionality at every step. Leadership requires the courage to stand against protectionist activities, even as it demands thoughtful approaches to the activities required of a church's mission in its community.

The practices and patterns highlighted in this last chapter are intended to protect assets, even as they enhance ministry. They are designed to lay the foundation, to ensure the presence of resources, needed for a congregation to do what it needs to do in its quest to align with God's purposes. Consider this book as a call for intentionality, a call to intentionally open individuals and churches to the work to which God calls them, a call to prepare, to work, to sacrifice, to give in ways that allow for sharing the good news. Even those of us with legal, financial, or business training aren't ready to say that finance and administration are fun. As aggressively as I caution against no intentionality in those areas, I equally warn against a sense that they are the place of real ministry. Business meetings in churches aren't really where the action should be. No one should be clamoring to find a place on trustees, the finance team, or staff parish. Real ministry happens with people. Finance and administrative practices are about empowerment, maximization, and unleashing of people to be in ministry with others.

If this book does nothing else, I hope it leads to greater intentionality in creating healthy practices that undergird strong ministries always reaching out to new people. It is always my hope that healthy people become healthy leaders, that holy people lead holy congregations.

CPSIA information can be obtained
at www.ICGtesting.com
Printed in the USA
LVOW13s0246110317

526844LV00005B/6/P